THE
CRY
GOD
HEARS

THE
CRY
GOD
HEARS

BARBARA J. YODER

Chosen

a division of Baker Publishing Group
Grand Rapids, Michigan

Published by Chosen Books
11400 Hampshire Avenue South
Bloomington, Minnesota 55438

Chosen Books is a division of
Baker Publishing Group, Grand Rapids, Michigan.

Printed in the United States of America

In keeping with biblical principles of creation stewardship, Baker Publishing Group advocates the responsible use of our natural resources. As a member of the Green Press Initiative, our company uses recycled paper when possible. The text paper of this book is comprised of 30% post-consumer waste.

green press
INITIATIVE

Library of Congress Cataloging-in-Publication Data

Yoder, Barbara J.
    The cry God hears— : and is waiting to answer / Barbara J. Yoder ; foreword by C. Peter Wagner.
      p.   cm.
    Includes bibliographical references.
    ISBN 978–0–8007–9500–9 (pbk. : alk. paper) 1. Jesus Christ—Kingdom. 2. Church. 3. People of God. 4. Christian life. 5. Mission of the church. I. Title.
    BT94.Y63   2011
    231.7'2—dc22

2010036891

CONTENTS

FOREWORD

IF YOU YEARN TO MOVE to a new level in fulfilling the destiny God has planned for you, this is the book you need. Barbara Yoder, a close friend over many, many years, is a woman of blunt realism. She insists on evaluating the situation in our world, in our nation, in our church and in ourselves with an eye that sees things as they really are. She does not live in some fantasy or a spiritual dream world. She refuses to fall into denial. She will not sugarcoat the pill.

Yet Barbara's view of today's reality is not one of despair. Her horizon is a horizon of victory! A new season is coming. God's plans reach far beyond our ordinary expectations. However, in order for us to move into the new, we must be willing to leave the old.

How do we do this? As you will see, Barbara makes the spine-tingling suggestion that we each write our own "book." Then she guides us through the process step-by-step. With each step we take, our lives will write a book that tells of God's faithfulness. For most of us, that book will be figurative. However, some of us may choose to keep a journal along the way—or perhaps even write a literal book—to detail our stories. But most of all, like those following Paul the apostle, our lives will evolve into a type of book, an epistle written by God. In a cry God hears, we will cry out for God's direction, discover His assignments and move forward into the future with Him. You will love the process!

Whenever we write our own "book," we need to lead up to a certain conclusion. *The Cry God Hears* does this, and its last chapter, "Kingdom Come," shows us the encouraging horizon of victory yet to come. Barbara tells each of us, "Your book will end well because the Kingdom endures and overcomes. You are now writing part of a bigger story." In order to make this a reality, she states that we must change from a Church paradigm to a Kingdom paradigm.

Changing paradigms? Yes! Here is how Barbara sees it: "Scripture is jam-packed with examples, one after another, of God breaking individuals and groups, even whole nations, out of their old paradigms." This is true, but the process is never easy. Barbara also reminds us that whenever we enter a new era, we will need to go through some form of travail. This is true because every time we contemplate a new paradigm, it begins to pull us out of the comfort zones the old paradigm provided.

Moving from our former Church paradigm to a new Kingdom paradigm will require us to open ourselves to certain mindsets that can easily stretch our comfort zones. I have given quite a bit of thought to this recently, and I would like to suggest three of these mindsets that every one of us would do well to consider, whether they represent radical paradigm shifts for us or not.

First, *we must keep the Church in biblical perspective.* I can attest that we have had a shortsighted view of the Church because I have shared in that shortsightedness. I felt that saving souls and building the Church was our primary goal. However, now I realize that the Kingdom of God is greater than the Church. Jesus never sent His disciples to preach the "Gospel of salvation" or the "Gospel of the Church." He always sent them to preach the "Gospel of the Kingdom." Theologically, the Church is not the Kingdom. And the Church is not a building. It is a people whose purpose is to release the Kingdom—the realm of God's rule and authority—into every sphere of life.

When we see the bigger picture, we soon begin to realize that the Church is not only the congregation that meets in a certain place, usually on Sundays, but that it fundamentally means "the people of God." They are the Church. And that means that they are the Church not only on Sunday, but also on the other six days of the week, in the workplace. There is truly a Church in the workplace because the people of God are there. A corollary of this is that what God's people do in the workplace can be just as valid a form of ministry as singing in the choir or pastoring a church.

Second, *we must take the Great Commission literally.* As we all know, Jesus told His disciples to go and make disciples of all the nations. Our old paradigm thinking led us to believe that we were supposed to go to all the nations and make as many individual disciples in them as possible. But the literal meaning is not that; it is to make the whole nation or social unit a follower of Christ. God told Adam and Eve that they were to take dominion of His creation (see Genesis 1:28), and He still expects His people to do that. Satan has had dominion over the nations for too long, and God expects us to turn things around. This is our dominion mandate!

Third, *we must be willing to reconsider our traditional eschatology.* I do not know about you, but those who trained me in the Christian faith taught me that the world was getting worse and worse. However, we were not to be concerned—when things became bad enough, all believers suddenly would be raptured from the world, and the Antichrist would take over. But obviously this traditional view of end-times eschatology no longer fits if we decide to take the Great Commission literally and obey the dominion mandate. We do not need an escapist eschatology; we need a victorious eschatology. Our task is to see that God's Kingdom comes and that our cities and nations get better and better, as Barbara Yoder projects.

You can depend on the fact that, as Barbara puts it, "God is doing something fresh in the world today." I know that you want to be a part of it. You do not want to be a spectator; you want to be a participant. As you move through this book, chapter by exhilarating chapter, it will capture your spirit with the assurance that victory can be won and that you can be one of those who lifts up a "cry God hears"!

C. Peter Wagner, Chancellor
Wagner Leadership Institute

ACKNOWLEDGMENTS

WRITING A BOOK IS, for me, an inimitable assignment from God dropped into the middle of an already busy and challenging life. This book was particularly challenging and unique. It was written partly out of my own journey to make sense of what I was experiencing, as well as what I observed as I traveled around this nation and the nations of the world. In its formation it is personal as well as corporate. The assignment emerged out of the chaos of transition and change.

I want to thank all the leaders with whom I interacted as I moved around the nation and the world; the leaders and people with whom I interacted regularly at home; and those on the journey with me.

Jane Campbell always bears with my agonizing and fulfilling journey of giving birth to the finished project, struggling to find words and concepts to express what I see and sense, as well as processing what I hear others saying, and then grounding it in God's Word. Kathryn Deering takes every word and chapter I write, weaving them into a tapestry demonstrating the beauty of a carefully crafted creative project, forming a potent message.

My heart is always to help others make sense of their lives in the midst of chaotic and confusing times. It is true that without God I can do nothing. But I also feel that without Jane and Kathryn, I cannot complete a book. So together, God, Jane and Kathryn form my threefold cord. From the bottom of my heart, thanks.

1

The Dilemma

WHAT IN THE WORLD is going on in the world? On every level—global, national, regional, local and individual—what used to be secure seems to have destabilized. Every week brings another batch of bad news. After absorbing it, we grapple with the repercussions and try to move back into the flow of normal life. But what does "normal life" mean anymore? Many of our efforts to restabilize go nowhere. Our assumptions and expectations about what is normal are being challenged at every turn.

In the United States, expectations for normal life used to include steady employment, or at least the solid hope of a future job. We also felt safe from physical threats most of the time. Terrorists lived in faraway countries, and we could go to the airport without having to navigate multiple layers of security. Not so long ago, we could expect to see Judeo-Christian morals play out in the marketplace and in legal affairs. We did not expect to have to contend against our own government for our unalienable rights. What on earth has happened to the old norms? Why is so much evil running wild?

Human life, of course, has always involved challenges and perplexities. We blame fallen human nature and Mother Nature, too. But something about this time is different. We seem to have entered a new era of some kind. It is as if we have turned a corner, and there is no turning back. We are beginning to recognize that we have a dilemma, and we do not know what to do next.

Is this sense of disconnect between the past and the present a figment of our imagination? Or does it point to a new reality?

A New Global Reality

Overwhelming threats of destruction now dominate our world—climate changes, economic chaos, terrorism, pandemic health menaces, biological and chemical weapons, globalization, with its resulting shifts in world power and wealth, and much more.[1] Not only are most of our leaders incapable of confronting the disconnect between what the world used to be and what it now is, they also cannot address the additional division that has opened up between what we believe (or used to believe) and what actually works. According to Joshua Ramo, author of *The Age of the Unthinkable*, leaders in today's world lack the language, the creativity and the revolutionary spirit they need to confront the current challenges. Blinded by power, position and prestige, leaders cannot assess the reality of the global situation. Thus, the future of the average person is in the hands of people who are bewildered by it.[2]

In other words, we are facing a new world, a new age, a new order of unprecedented proportions. The situation calls for new strategies and new frameworks from people who can see beyond what has worked in the past and who have the ability to leave behind old models and look at things with new vision. With revitalized vision, people can see overwhelming circumstances in a new and fresh way.

But you know as well as I do that human solutions will only add to the chaos. We need God. We need His protection, His strategies, His wisdom. We need His Kingdom to come—the sooner the better!

I would say that this new global reality is a "perfect storm" and a perfect opportunity for the Body of Christ to rally under their King to bring in the Kingdom of God as never before.

Pivotal Moment

Whatever we do, we cannot afford to ignore the situation. In fact, no man, woman or child will be able to ignore it. Whether you can detect the unnerving invisible undercurrents or will need to be hit with the proverbial two-by-four before noticing them, you will not be able to hide your head in the sand or escape to another planet. You have already boarded the *Titanic,* and it has now struck the iceberg. That rushing sound you hear is icy seawater filling the hold. You may have had plans for your future, but they are now changing. Have you grasped it yet? The ship you trusted in is sinking fast. The miracles you need will not look like anything you have ever seen before.

I remember my first moments of awareness that something unsettling was happening. I was walking to one of my favorite restaurants to join friends for a relaxed evening of good Italian food and camaraderie. As I walked down the street, past familiar establishments and people in good spirits, I started to feel as if I were in a foreign land. Talk about disconnect—what a strange feeling. What was this vague sense of uneasiness? Where did this indefinable apprehension come from?

It reminded me a little of the way I felt when the Twin Towers fell on September 11, 2001, although my shock and fear on 9/11 were the direct result of seeing what was happening on my television screen, and my feelings were shared by just about everyone. This time, however, people on the street seemed oblivious, and no traumatic event had occurred.

Over the next few days and weeks, I could not shake the feeling that I had lost my mooring point. Regardless of where I went—home, work, church, traveling, with or without other people—I felt removed from the scene, as if I no longer understood the world in which I lived. I felt like a stranger. It began to dawn on me that something very fundamental must have changed. Somewhere in the universe, someone must have switched the channel without telling me.

I needed to figure out what to do next. I needed to know if I was crazy or if others were experiencing the same thing. I talked to friends, and sure enough, some of them (but not all) were experiencing something similar. They were as incapable of defining it as I was, but they had noticed a shift, too.

Some time later, my ministry hosted a conference at which a national leader was speaking. I took notice when he said, "Never in my entire life have I received as many communications from pastors stating that they don't know what to do anymore. 'Nothing is working,' they are telling me. 'The programs, strategies, methodologies and techniques that used to yield such amazing results have all lost their fizz. None of them are coming close to producing the results they used to. In fact, they don't work at all.' These pastors are baffled and confused. They don't know what to do or where to go and do it. Furthermore, it seems that God isn't even speaking to them much about anything. They don't know what's going on."

There it was again, an undefined shift from all that was familiar. Nothing was working for me, either. I was feeling increasingly uncomfortable, out of sync, exhausted. I was not enjoying this time of flux. It was so hard to see—I felt as if I were wearing dark glasses at night. But whatever was going on, I could choose to be a spectator on the sidelines or a participant who would influence the unfolding of the next steps.

Oblivious?

Because most people do not evaluate the underlying dynamic of this age in which they live, they do not discover this simple truth: It is an age now characterized by uncertainty. They keep thinking that they should be able to make their feelings of unsettledness just go away, so they try to fix the blame on somebody or something in order to "fix" things. They change jobs, careers, churches, friends, houses, spouses, activities—whatever seems to provide a change. Does it work? Of course not. We are dealing with something bigger than that.

You and I were destined to live in this present time. God has put us right where we find ourselves. He has equipped us, and He will strengthen us to overcome all obstacles. He will help us endure hardship with unspeakable joy, because He wants to release great glory through us. This time of uncertain footing brings us to the threshold of the days we have only dreamed about. We just did not expect them to unfold like this.

Our circumstances cause us to cry out to God—and that is exactly what He wants us to do. We will never step into our full destiny if we do not embrace the life He has given us now. Compelled by our helplessness, we go straight to the top for divine intervention and assistance. We realize that we must surrender to His Lordship over our situation as we look to Him for our unknown future.

The future calls for changes in us as individuals, changes in how we see the world, how we educate and train ourselves to act, whom we align ourselves with and how we build a faith that will see us through. In the face of crises and very real dangers, the people of God must become resilient, faith-filled carriers of hope and love. Only with God's help can we overcome our fear of pain and embrace adversity, recognizing that it is the entrance to the Kingdom of God. As Acts 14:22 says: "We must through many tribulations enter the kingdom of God." Only with Him can we find that mind-blowing joy that becomes strength in the face of weakness.

When God challenged Ezra to begin the long journey back to Jerusalem, the scribe was overwhelmed. The way ahead was fraught with danger, and he lacked confidence about his ability to safely lead others all that way:

> Then I proclaimed a fast there at the river of Ahava, that we might humble ourselves before our God, to seek from Him the right way for us and our little ones and all our possessions. For I was ashamed to request of the king an escort of soldiers and horsemen to help us against the enemy on the road, because we had spoken to the king, saying, "The hand of our God is upon all those for good who seek Him, but His power and His wrath are against all those who forsake Him." So we fasted and entreated our God for this, and He answered our prayer.
>
> *EZRA 8:21–23*

Ezra and the people cried out to God in their uncertainty and desperation, and God answered fully. Not only did He keep them safe all the long way back to Jerusalem from Babylon, He also secured their future there, leading them to further reestablish the city as their own—and His.

In a time such as the one we find ourselves in today, let's encourage each other to cry out to God like that. The book you hold in your hands is my effort to help you know what to say.

2

The New Book

FEVERISHLY I WAS WRITING, taking advantage of every second. I had a tight book deadline to meet. Suddenly the condo phone rang. That was strange because it was not my house or my phone. I was hiding out to accomplish my assignment, and the only people who knew where I was were the owners of the condo. There was no answering machine to field the call, and I did not have the time to talk. I did not want to answer the phone, but since a call was so unexpected, I decided I had better answer it. *Who knows, it might be something really important*, I thought. Besides, I had that sense that something was up.

I picked up the phone and heard a familiar voice. Bishop Bill Hamon was on the other end. Quickly dispensing with the usual mannerly greetings, he got right to the point: "I want you to come over to my office tomorrow morning. There is a word I want to prophesy to you."

That was not his modus operandi, not his usual style. I had never known him to call and say something like that, although he had prophesied to me several times over the years. In the past, Bishop Hamon had always prophesied in the context of ministering to those on his board or when he was speaking in my church. Never a personal phone call out of the clear blue sky, so I knew it was important.

Someone who prophesies to you is telling you what he or she believes God is saying to you. Prophecy is either a gift of the Spirit or a word from a prophet in the ministry office of the prophet (see 1 Corinthians 12:10; Ephesians 4:11). When it is a gift of the Holy Spirit, it edifies or builds you up; it comforts or exhorts you and stirs you up (see 1 Corinthians 14:3). In addition, prophecy coming from a prophet may give you direction and correction. I had no idea what Bishop Hamon might say to me when he prophesied, but I knew that deadline or not, I had better show up the next day, as he asked.

Writing like crazy, I finished out that day without ruminating further over what he might say. I was too busy getting the book written. I wrote until I ran out of time, went swimming in the Gulf of Mexico to wash away the intensity of the day's work and then headed off for supper.

I was writing about death being the entryway to a new beginning. The book was called *The Overcomer's Anointing: God's Plan to Use Your Darkest Hour As Your Greatest Spiritual Weapon* (Chosen, 2009), and part of the theme was about how old things need to die before we can be delivered to the doorstep of something new. I was not yet able to articulate this idea well. I had simply begun to understand that massive changes were occurring across society and in people's lives personally and corporately. Many people, me included, were experiencing the death of many things. I was writing about the sense of grief, loss, uncertainty and insecurity, even anxiety, that had closed in on people. God seemed to be saying, "I have pulled the plug on who you have been, what you have done, whom you have done it with, how you have done it, viewed it, experienced it before."

I was immersed in this topic of "ending," and that evening when I stopped to relax and regroup for the next day, I still had much to write. Now, added to my writing schedule, I had the morning appointment with Bishop Hamon. I was intrigued that he felt he needed to give me a word when I was dying to so much, not only from a writing standpoint, but personally. I was aware that something about my ministry life had ended, yet I knew that endings always lead to new beginnings. I just wished I knew more about what the future held. Immersed in the ending, I was totally muddled over what the next thing would be.

At times I felt like a cat who had run playfully inside a paper bag, only to have someone quickly staple the opening shut. Now I could not get out of what I thought was a great place to play. I was stuck. At other times I felt like a mouse that the cat had caught. Although I was at death's door, the cat would not stop playing with me and get it over with. The cat just would not let me die, so I had ended up in what seemed like a perpetual state of dying. I wanted to say, "Just let this poor soul die!" Have you ever felt that way when you come to the end of all that is familiar?

"That Chapter Is Closed"

Anticipating my meeting with Bishop Hamon, I was more curious than I was nervous. Bishop Hamon is an honorable and godly man, one who seeks to build and establish. I trust him, and I knew that since he had called me to come, he must have something important to say. He is like a father in my life.

The bishop's office is an experience in and of itself. As I walked in, I drew away from a huge stuffed lion that looked as though it was jumping out of the wall on my left. His office is full of items that a person's imagination can get lost in. There are funny puzzle-like illusions on his desk. The room speaks of the wonderful uniqueness of his personality. Bishop Hamon himself is an experience, an amazingly diverse, gifted, wise, learned, yet down-to-earth leader. He is a true original—the only bishop his age that I know of who has fractured his collarbone in his early seventies while driving a four-wheeler at full throttle.

I walked past the lion to meet with him. We chatted briefly with the usual friendly icebreakers: "How are you? What's been going on?" Then Bishop Hamon began to prophesy to me:

> And the Lord says, "Daughter, this July has finished a whole era of your life, and August has started a whole new dimension and whole new era of your life." And the Lord says, "That chapter is closed, and that book is closed. We are opening up another book of your life and we are starting on a new way. . . . Watch for the new adventure; watch the new advancement; watch the new relationships; watch the new things that are about to happen, because you are going to feel like you have just started out all over again. You will be filled with a sense of joy and expectancy and excitement. . . ."

Wow, just what I had been writing about! Bishop Hamon did not know what I was working on. Something *had* ended. You could call it an era, a chapter or a book that had been completed. Now, speaking for the Lord, Bishop Hamon was saying that something new was being set in motion: a new book, a new way, a new adventure.

I focused on the words *a whole new era*. They caught my attention. I had been preaching and writing about death, explaining how God was bringing each of us, as well as the Church, to a place of death so that He could bring forth something new. I had felt like a pioneer forging into new territory, preaching a message that I had not yet heard anyone else preaching. Yet it kept ringing inside my spirit like a bell. I thought of Hemingway's book *For Whom the Bell Tolls*. The bells were ringing inside me. There had been a death and even a funeral. I had not fully comprehended or processed what was happening, yet I could not stop the ringing. I knew I had to risk stepping out on a limb to say what God was asking me to say. I felt a bit like John the Baptist heralding his message in the wilderness. *But he was right on,* I told myself. *What if I am way off, way out there and missing it, missing God's message?* I felt as if I were backing into new territory blindfolded.

Pick Up the New Book

Shortly after that week, I was ministering to a group of people when out of my mouth came the words, "God is waiting for us to pick up the new book. He has shut the completed book from which we have been living and has placed a new one in our hands. Not only has God placed a new book in our hands; He wants us to consciously, with our wills, set down the old book that is now filled and finished. Set it down. Put it away. Shelve it. For that book is done. It is over with. It contains no more pages from which to live."

I went on to say, "You all have your Bibles with you. Pretend that your Bible is the new book. Grab it and hold it up. Declare that God has placed a new book in your hands and that you will now live out of the new book. Declare that the old one is over. The pages of your new book are empty. Not even the first chapter or the first page has been written. You need to write in it. You will write your book by launching out into the deep, by taking a leap of faith and stepping into the new."

I did not really know what I was saying. I could not understand what it meant. Neither did anyone else. We just sensed it was right, that it was what God was speaking.

A shout exploded from the people as they took their Bibles, pretending that they were the new, blank books, and lifted them high. Somehow we knew we were in a new book and that the old book was finished. We had completed an era of our lives.

I kept seeing that the new book had nothing written in it yet. The words "Chapter 1" were there, but beyond that, nothing was inscribed on the first page. Every subsequent page was totally blank. I kept hearing the Lord say, "This generation will write the book," and I felt He meant those in the Church who are alive today, regardless of their current age in years. Writing the new book would be an intergenerational assignment. Together as well as individually, we would author it by corporately intertwining our lives, each of us gifts of God to one another and to this era, forging the book through our joint contributions as we journeyed into the new.

But what were we talking about? What *is* this new book?

Books and More Books

What is a book, scripturally speaking? Before I surveyed the Bible to answer this question, I had no idea there were so many variations of "books" identified in Scripture.

For example, I found "the *book* of the genealogy of Adam" (Genesis 5:1, emphasis added). The Lord instructed Moses, "Write this for a memorial in the *book*" (Exodus 17:14, emphasis added). Exodus 24:7 refers to "the Book of the Covenant." Moses said to God in Exodus 32:32, "Blot me out of Your book which You have written." (This was before we had the Bible, so the book Moses refers to is not the same as Scripture.) Numbers 5:23 mentions a book in which the priests wrote curses, and Numbers 21:14 mentions a "Book of the Wars of the LORD."

Of course, we also have the Book of the Law, which Joshua called "the Book of the Law of Moses" (see Deuteronomy 28:58, 61;

Joshua 8:31; 23:6; 2 Kings 14:6; 2 Chronicles 25:4; Nehemiah 8:1).
Joshua himself wrote in a book called "the Book of the Law of God"
(see Joshua 24:26; Nehemiah 8:18). I also read that "Samuel explained
to the people the behavior of royalty, and wrote it in a *book* and laid
it up before the LORD" (1 Samuel 10:25, emphasis added).

David wanted the children of Judah to learn the Song of the
Bow, which was written in the Book of Jasher (see 2 Samuel 1:18).
The Book of Jasher (or Jashar in some translations) was "an ancient
collection of verse, now lost, which described great events in the
history of Israel. The book contained Joshua's poetic address to the
sun and the moon at the battle of Gibeon (Joshua 10:12–13) and
the 'Song of the Bow,' which is David's lament over the death of Saul
and Jonathan" (2 Samuel 1:17–27).[1]

I found book after book mentioned in the Bible. Scripture goes
on to speak of "the book of the acts of Solomon" (see 1 Kings 11:41),
which was the book of the chronicles of the kings of Israel and of
Judah. When Hilkiah, the high priest, found the Book of the Law in
the house of the Lord, reading the book brought great consternation and potential calamity on King Josiah and all the people (see
2 Kings 22:3–16). When this book was read and it was determined
that their fathers had not "obeyed the words of this book, to do
according to all that is written concerning us" (verse 13), the king
tore his clothes and repented, after which Huldah prophesied that
the judgment of God would be delayed until after his death because
of his tender heart toward God. Josiah proceeded to lead the people
of Judah to repent of all their idolatrous ways, and God withheld
judgment as a result. The Book of the Law had told them about the
consequences of their actions, and then Huldah had prophesied
how they were to respond to the terms of the Law.

Searching further, I recalled that the decree of Esther on Purim
was written in a book (see Esther 9:32). Job also cried out in reference to a book:

Oh, that my words were written!
Oh, that they were inscribed in a *book*!
That they were engraved on a rock
With an iron pen and lead, forever!
For I know that my Redeemer lives,
And He shall stand at last on the earth;
And after my skin is destroyed, this I know,
That in my flesh I shall see God,
Whom I shall see for myself,
And my eyes shall behold, and not another.
How my heart yearns within me!

JOB 19:23–27, EMPHASIS ADDED

Job's words captured my attention. Something about the significance of his words caused Job to *cry out*, longing for them to be inscribed in a book. I was beginning to see a connection. Would the blank pages of our new books record our heart cries to God? David had instructed that his tears be put in a bottle, then he queried the Lord, "Are they not in Your *book*?" (Psalm 56:8, emphasis added). In Psalm 69:28 David referred to the "book of the living," making the assumption that, on the basis of righteousness, names could be added or subtracted. David also mentioned a book in which God had recorded the details of David's formation before he was even born (see Psalm 139:16).

Some books capture significant events and hold memories sacrosanct, making them indelible and tamper proof, untouchable. Some books store words that are sealed and cannot be understood until the right person reads them at the right time (see Isaiah 29:11, 18). Some books contain words that lay out the future of nations. God instructed Jeremiah to write in a book all the words that He had spoken to him (see Jeremiah 25:13; 30:2).

So we see that books can record significant utterances. Malachi 3:16 refers to a "book of remembrance." Scribes wrote chronicles of their kings' deeds and the deeds of those who interacted with the kings. To say God has a book of remembrance does not mean that He needs a physical book to help Him remember everything, of course. He does not require memory prompts. But we often need them, and picturing God's "book of remembrance" helps us remember that our deeds are chronicled before Him and that He will remember them at the Day of Judgment.

Scripture mentions many other such heavenly books. "Ten thousand times ten thousand stood before Him. The court was seated, and the books were opened" (Daniel 7:10). "I went to the angel and said to him, 'Give me the little book.' And he said to me, 'Take and eat it; and it will make your stomach bitter, but it will be as sweet as honey in your mouth'" (Revelation 10:9–10). "Then Moses returned to the LORD and said, 'Oh, these people have committed a great sin, and have made for themselves a god of gold! Yet now, if You will forgive their sin—but if not, I pray, blot me out of Your book which You have written.'" (Exodus 32:31–32). David prayed, "Let them be blotted out of the book of the living, and not be written with the righteous" (Psalm 69:28). Jesus told His disciples, "Nevertheless do not rejoice in this, that the spirits are subject to you, but rather rejoice because your names are written in heaven" (Luke 10:20).

Choose Your Book

By definition, a book is simply a set of handwritten, printed or blank pages fastened together along one side and encased between protective covers. A book can serve many purposes. It can record factual information, including information of a private, secret nature that belongs only to the owner of the book. No one else knows the contents or is aware of them. Our blank books can become such a register of our lives in this new era, a record in our minds (and for some of us, on paper) of the journey God leads us on into our future.

A book can contain a set of prescribed standards or rules on which decisions are based. I believe God has thrown out the religious, legalistic rulebook from the previous era, a rulebook that bound us to tradition and religion. It was not based on the Living Word of God and was therefore replaceable.

A book may be a source of knowledge or understanding. This book we will write with our lives (and perhaps with our pens) will record the unfolding of our understanding about this new era we are now entering. It will contain our accumulated experience, knowledge, understanding and skills—whatever we learn that can be used to solve problems and perform tasks.

This book probably will not be a literal book at all for most of you. However, the image of a book captures the idea that you are entering into a new story, a new unfolding of something that has heretofore been hidden from you. You cannot know what that story is until you enter your next season . . . the unfolding story of your life.

Our books (the unfolding story of our lives) will form a record, a memorial, a journal. They will contain plans, strategies, results and records of what God has said to us, instructions He has given and will yet give us. Our books, which may be literal or figurative or both, will contain a record of everything that transpires in this new era. Think about Lucy opening that wardrobe door in *The Chronicles of Narnia*. Once she stepped through that door, a whole new world opened up for her. As you step into this new era, imagine what will open up for you.

Interesting phrases use the word *book*, such as *to bring to book*, which means "to demand an explanation from" or "to call to account." It is a fact that each of us will be "brought to book" or called to account for how we live our lives in this new era.

Another phrase we use is *I know him like a book*. In other words, a book can represent complete knowledge. Or someone can *throw the book* at us, meaning that the contents of a book can be turned into charges against us. We can be reprimanded or punished based on what has been written in a book.

Book can also be used as a verb. To *book* something means "to cause it to be set aside in advance for one's personal use or possession." In other words, a person is claiming something by calling it their own ahead of time. To *book* also means "to register in a book, to enroll, to inscribe, to set down, to write down." It is related to remembering things too important to forget by writing them down.

To Write a Book

Writing a book presumes a commitment of time and personal involvement. Whether you literally keep a journal or write a book, or whether you write an "open book" with your daily life as you follow God, it will take time and energy to write it well.

When you and I literally write a book or journal, we can write at our own pace, according to our availability and desire. However, actual writing requires that we be much more exact than when we simply retain a fact in our minds. Any book that I write conveys my voice; your book will also convey your voice. And when someone touches your book, that person touches you. A literal book is a tangible expression of who you are and what you are like.

God instructed Habakkuk to write the vision. We do not know exactly how he recorded it, but he said, "Then the LORD answered me and said: 'Write the vision and make it plain on tablets, that he may run who reads it'" (Habakkuk 2:2). For all of us, at least going that far with pen and paper is a wonderful idea—writing out the vision God placed on our hearts once we cried out to Him.

God may instruct some of you to write even more, and for you, it will be good to know that a generation of people will be able to take what you write and run with it. When you literally write what you see and hear in a book (or a journal), it will take not only you, but also others to the next place. When you commit things to paper, you are registering your intent, charting your course, reserving your space and laying down on paper where you intend to go. By writing the vision, you will determine your future. You might also help others see a way into the future through these challenging times.

God is saying that He has put an empty book into our hands. For most of us it will not be a literal book. However, it does mean that something marvelous and mysterious is about to unfold. We are in a brand-new era. This era is likely to be decades long, perhaps as much as forty years. It will not be merely a day or a fleeting season. And now we can *choose* what will be in that book—choose it, walk it out and maybe even write it down.

Moses said to Joshua:

> Now therefore, fear the LORD, serve Him in sincerity and in truth, and put away the gods which your fathers served on the other side of the River and in Egypt. Serve the LORD! And if it seems evil to you to serve the LORD, choose for yourselves this day whom you will serve, whether the gods which your fathers served that were on the other side of the River, or the gods of the Amorites, in whose land you dwell. But as for me and my house, we will serve the LORD.
>
> *JOSHUA 24:14–15*

God challenges each of us with similar words. Choose whom you will serve. Record your choice in your book. Who will your master and lord be? What will you do in this next era? You could say it this way in the modern vernacular:

> If you decide that it's a bad thing to worship GOD, then choose a god you'd rather serve—and do it today. Choose one of the gods your ancestors worshiped from the country beyond The River, or one of the gods of the Amorites, on whose land you're now living. As for me and my family, we'll worship GOD.
>
> *JOSHUA 24:15, THE MESSAGE*

More Questions Than Answers

We are in a new time and season, and each of us has been handed a blank book. What will we write in our book? What are we breaking through to? Is this our agenda or God's?

What about this brand-new era? Who are we supposed to be? What are we supposed to do? What other people should we team up with? Who are the players who will go with us? How can we find the best and the brightest, those who have readied themselves for the highest purposes of God?

Do we have a deadline? What will it take to finish the job? Can we accomplish it in the time we have left? If we cannot, who will take the baton from us, and how will we prepare them?

Maybe our book is supposed to take shape initially as a book of *questions*—lots of questions, tons of questions! What question or questions will be *answered* by our book? What questions should we ask to find the answer to the original or seminal question? What is the ultimate purpose, the highest glory we are reaching for? What process must we go through to grasp it? What steps need to be taken? What obstacles stand before us? What land mines are hidden on our path to blow us up and stop us dead in our tracks? Where have sewer holes been left open, ready to swallow us up as we stumble into them?

Who is our audience? Who are our witnesses? What will they be looking for as we strive to answer the questions?

Why are there so many questions to ask? Why should we answer them? What if we fail to answer them? Will our answers change anything or anyone? Will they change the future? Does anyone really care if the future is changed?

If I write in the book, will it be worth it? How do I find out what my book is supposed to be about? Should it even be written? Will anyone read it? Why should anyone read it? And why do I even want to write it? Am I equipped to write it? What is the next step?

The next step for all of us who are writing a book with our lives is to cry out to God, seek Him desperately and do what He instructs us to do as we move into the future with Him. Some of us will also take the additional step of chronicling the path He leads us on in a journal, or perhaps even a full-length book. Whatever steps we may take along those lines, crying out to Him is the first step.

A New Era

We are not living in the world we used to live in. We are in a new period of time, a new book, and its pages are for the most part still empty. What is different about today? How are we different? How is the world different? What has changed from the previous era? What has shifted? How did it happen?

You and I certainly do not have all the answers, so we do not know how to write in this new book! But get your pen out anyway. The just shall live by faith (see Habakkuk 2:4; Galatians 3:11). Watch, look and listen. Stand in the watchtower, the place of the watchman, looking out, peering vigilantly across the landscape of the current era, looking up to see what God wants to do and looking down to see what you should write in your book (whether a figurative book, literal or both).

Our future is being transformed before us. The seeming brilliance of the former days is slipping away from our sight. Those days are gone. Massive changes have stolen our breath away. The previous book, the previous era, is now finished, completed, closed. Pick up the new book and begin to write. Chapter 1, open and empty, invites you. You are a historymaker like Joshua, who wrote a new book as he went treading through the land, taking it piece by piece. He held on to his hope throughout the entire wilderness era, when hope was in a stranglehold. Then, when the time came for a new era, he was ready. Not only did he have the strength of a warrior to conquer the Promised Land, he also had the eloquence of a scribe to write the story of the new era as he followed the Spirit of God step after step, day after day, year after year.

You and I are prisoners of hope, having been chained by the God of hope. We are picking up pen and paper, scribbling out our future in dark times. Our names are already written in God's book; our inward parts and everything about us has already been recorded in God's book. Our destiny is set. Will you believe in His vision and pursue it with passion? Will you write it and make it plain with your life, your words and your actions? Will you pick up your pen, so to speak, and put it to paper to record what happens?

3

It Is in Your Hands

So—YOU ARE THE PROUD OWNER of a new, blank book! In fact, you cannot let it go. That thing is glued onto your hands. You are like a little child trying to get rid of a wad of sticky tape, transferring it from one hand to the other. You have no idea what to do with it, but you cannot get rid of it. And if you are smart, you will not try very hard to drop it, because it is the unwritten account of your new era. If you let go of it, you will be turning your back on your future.

Something about this book intrigues you. It may be filled with danger, and yet something draws you into its mystery. You open the book—i.e., your imagination about the next season of your life—to sneak a quick look. Sure enough, nothing has been written yet. Blank pages stare you in the face. What is the attraction? Maybe it is that God Himself is inviting you to write a new story and record a history as it unfolds, describing visions, plans, strategies, successes, failures, triumphs, defeats. That sounds like an adventure. Perhaps your uneventful life is about to get interesting. What will your next season look like?

Wait a second . . . this is unnerving. Maybe you would rather retreat to the familiar ground you have just covered. You look over your shoulder, but all you can see there is another book. That one used to be blank, but now it is finished, filled up. It is now a record of the past.

So you have entered a new era. You may or may not have picked up on the preliminary indications, but now you are beginning to understand. The prophet Isaiah quoted God as saying, "See, the former things have taken place, and new things I declare; before they spring into being I announce them to you" (Isaiah 42:9, NIV).

Will you accept this challenge? From this time on, how will your story unfold? What will you be writing in your blank book?

Spiritual Breakthrough

It is not only individuals holding new, blank books. The nations of the world are holding new books, too. Something has shifted. The old books have been completed and closed as tightly as the door of a safe. We have a simple choice: Either we dig in our heels and refuse to move, individually, corporately and nationally, or we ask, "What must I do now?"

The new era requires spiritual breakthrough for us to begin "writing." Years ago I wrote a book called *The Breaker Anointing* (Regal, 2004). It describes spiritual breakthrough based on the implications of one of the names of God, the "Breaker." When I wrote it, the concept of breakthrough was relatively new. Since then, it has become commonplace, to the point that it can seem like meaningless jargon. However, it may be time to revisit the word.

One dictionary definition of *breakthrough* is "an offensive thrust that penetrates and carries an invading force beyond a defensive line in warfare." Note that breakthrough is part of an offense; it is not a defensive action. In other words, breakthrough is active, not passive. Of course, breakthrough implies that something has been broken. In particular, it involves breaking through and past an obstacle that stands between a person and a goal. Notably, most breakthroughs are "suddenlies." A breakthrough is a sudden advance, especially in knowledge or technique, as in a medical breakthrough, for instance.

The prophet Micah used the idea this way:

One who breaks open the way will go up before them;
    they will break through the gate and go out.
    Their king will pass through before them,
    the LORD at their head.
        MICAH 2:13, NIV

Something has to be broken *out of* as well as *into*. The one breaking through must move out of a confined, constricted place into larger, more expansive territory. Because people generally do not like adversity, they prefer to think of breakthrough as breaking out of something hard and difficult into a place of victory, ease, comfort and happiness. Biblically, that is far from the truth. Breakthrough is an ever-evolving process, one that involves increasing levels of difficulty until the force breaking through reaches the summit of the mountain it was assigned to conquer.

Consider Joshua. He had been at Moses' side until the day Moses died. On that day, a forty-year era ended; a book was closed. Moses had led the Israelites out of Egypt and through the wilderness. Miraculous intervention had brought one breakthrough after another, from escaping Egypt to crossing the Red Sea to surviving in the wilderness. Moses' story became the literal books of Exodus,

37

Leviticus, Numbers and Deuteronomy. When he died, that era was complete. A generation closed out.

Joshua walked with Moses throughout the whole journey. When Moses died, God said to Joshua, "Moses My servant is dead. Now therefore, arise, go over this Jordan, you and all this people, to the land which I am giving to them—the children of Israel" (Joshua 1:2). God gave Joshua a new book, and it was blank. And He appointed Joshua to lead the way in writing it. Joshua knew he would need God's help to fulfill the vision God had set before him. The past era was fulfilled, and the old books were closed. Moses had died, and Joshua was entering a new era without him.

Joshua looked out over the tents of Israel. Canaan was almost within sight on the far side of the river, but so were their foes. Joshua now had to figure out how to get the job done. His task was as much of a challenge as Moses' had been. Joshua embraced the challenge.

Like Joshua, when we say yes to our new, blank book of the future, we must incorporate what we have learned in past campaigns and come to a realistic assessment of our capabilities. You and I must evaluate ourselves and our past and ask ourselves some questions that will help us move ahead into victory.

Evaluate Your Past History

Why do we want to evaluate our past? So that we can discover those things that we want to carry into our future—things like treasures, valuable life lessons and character development, for example. Evaluating what we should leave in the past and what we should carry forward with us is one way we can be intentional about our future. Jesus said, "Therefore every teacher of the law who has been instructed about the kingdom of heaven is like the owner of a house who brings out of his storeroom new treasures as well as old" (Matthew 13:52, NIV).

What have you gleaned from your previous life experiences,

both good and bad, easy and difficult? What have you learned about God, yourself, others, the dynamics of relationships and life itself? In what ways have these experiences enlarged you, and where have they diminished you? Which life lessons will help you move forward? Which ones may hinder you? In what way have your life experiences contributed to the formation of habits, routines, attitudes or outlooks? Do you need to change anything? Do you need to leave some things or some people behind? (This does not mean there is something wrong with those people; it simply means they are not part of your new assignment for whatever reason.)

Who Am I?

You also need to ask yourself, *Who am I?* This is not a simple question. It requires thoughtful reflection and deliberation. Other important questions would be:

Where have I come from? How did I grow up? What was my family of origin (race, ethnicity, nationality, position in life, financial situation, family strengths and weaknesses)? What made that unique? What neighborhoods did I live in? What kind of schools did I attend? Who were my friends? What was I good at? What was I not good at? How was I affirmed? How was I put down or rejected? How did I excel? Where did I seem to fail, falter or feel fearful? Was I a leader or a follower?

What is my level of education and my specialty? Am I better at seeing the big picture or the little details? Am I a motivator, an igniter who works best with large groups casting vision and releasing passion? Or am I a disciple-coach whose heart is more to see people change at a personal level?

How have I turned out? What is my personality? Am I extroverted (outgoing, talkative) or introverted (shy, quiet)? Do people gravitate to me for direction and advice? Or do I look to others and follow them?

What are my talents (aptitudes, gifts, abilities, endowments)? What is my passion—what do I love to do? What would I do if I could do anything in the world and money was not a problem? What energizes me and puts life into me? When am I in my element? (Our element is comprised of both what we excel at and what we love to do.)

Do I know what God has called me to do with my life? Have I discovered my spiritual calling? What has God said about my life? What vision, assignment has He given me? How has He equipped me? What are my predominant spiritual gifts? In what ways are people most frequently affected when I express my gifts? Whom has He assigned me to work alongside? With whom am I aligned, spiritually speaking?

As I write this list of questions for us to ask ourselves, I think about my family. I have an older sister and a younger brother. In some ways, we are alike, yet each of us is unique. No one quality or experience has made us who we are today; our life experiences have combined with our individual personalities to equip each of us to do what God has called us to do. We share a common experience of family warmth, mental ability and encouragement, as well as an orientation toward helping those who are less fortunate. We care about other people because we grew up that way. Each of us has grown to excel at what we do. My sister is an amazing organizer, a helper, someone who comes alongside others to assist them. My brother is a skilled scientific researcher. I provide spiritual leadership and creativity. Each of us has our own book to write, our future to forge, a destiny to fulfill.

Chapter by Chapter

As you and I start to write in our blank books with our lives, it will be with the realization that our unfolding story is but a small, yet significant part of a larger whole. God, the current society and the times in which we live will all mold our story. It will be a record of our history from this moment forward in this emerging era.

Writing in a blank book is not something that only a select few people should do. It is for you and me, ordinary people who are forging our signatures into the earthen realm into which we have been born. You will write the history of your breakthroughs. How will you capture God's promises? How will you handle the baton that has been passed to you? As you walk these things out, the pages of your book will begin to fill.

We know what Joshua did with the charge that he inherited from Moses. Will you and I be equally faithful in executing our individual charges? Though most of us will not have the far-reaching significance Joshua had, in our own time and place we do have a charge for the sphere of assignment God has given to us.

Can you imagine what Joshua must have been thinking when God spoke to him about what he was supposed to do next? The people of Israel had been wandering around the wilderness for forty years, and their journey seemed to end up nowhere. Then overnight, Joshua was delivered to the door of the Promised Land.

God spoke to him and gave him the charge, the mandate, to go into Canaan and conquer it. God said, in essence, "Joshua, get up and cross the Jordan River [and since this was the highest point of the flood season, the river was impassable]. Take all the people with you [a huge bunch]. Every place you step down, every spot your foot comes down upon, I will give that piece of the territory to you" (see Joshua 1:3). In other words, God was saying, "It is your turn now, Joshua. Go ahead. Step up to the plate and hit a home run." Three times God told Joshua to "be strong and courageous." Yet considering the magnitude of the task, His directions were sparse, just enough to kick-start the process. Joshua would need supernatural faith to execute his charge from God.

When God places a new book in your hands, it will seem as

though you have just barely enough direction. Like Joshua, you will have to start walking, working and writing in your book by faith. Somehow, you will have to keep hearing God's voice so that you can penetrate the walls of opposition that will surely be in your way.

Joshua probably had cheerleaders, but he definitely had naysayers, too, those who thought this new adventure was a joke. The first wall he had to break through was the initial resistance of hardheartedness, unbelief, consternation, confusion and doubt. He had to take a step forward into the unknown even when he felt it was crazy. He had to come up with creative new ways of doing things. He had to make sure he had the right team of people around him. With each of those steps, Joshua began to write his book. Page by page, he began to move into his future, into the Promised Land.

So it is with you and me. Every time my assignment has shifted, I have felt blank, lost, confused, at times even helpless. Many times, I have thought the challenge was just too big. Yet every time I have taken that first step, it is as if a crack in the window shade allows a shaft of light to shed light on my next step. It is not much light, just enough to take one more step. Every time we launch out into the unknown with God, we can expect the right amount of illumination. We must find the light and then walk in it.

This "new book" you are writing with your life (and for a few of you, perhaps also with your pen) is not your idea. It is God's. When God initiates something, you can bank on the fact that He will work in you to complete it. All you have to do is follow Him persistently. "There has never been the slightest doubt in my mind that the God who started this great work in you would keep at it and bring it to a flourishing finish on the very day Christ Jesus appears" (Philippians 1:6, THE MESSAGE).

Changes and Challenges

I live in Michigan, a state that faces great challenges. The bottom has dropped out of the economy, and our unemployment rate remains far too high. The Big Three, as they call the auto giants, Ford, GM and Chrysler, have been struggling to survive. The economic engine of the state has changed. Quite abruptly, one book closed and another appeared. How will the state of Michigan write its future? Similar changes are happening around the nation and in the nations of the world. Life is no longer the way it used to be. The changes have thrust a new book into each of our hands.

What is your assignment in this new era? That is what you will write your book about. Please understand that this does not have to be some grandiose, international, high-level, top-secret assignment. Perhaps as a teacher, your assignment will be to influence your students in such a way that they are transformed and equipped to walk into their future. Perhaps as a parent, your assignment will be to spend time with your kids, giving them the tools they will need to grow up, carefully helping to mold their characters and identify their own assignments, training and nurturing them accordingly. If you are a CEO, your task may be to envision the future and then carefully craft your organization in such a way that it can shift successfully into the future.

From the individual to the corporate world, from the Church to secular society, from the family to the community, from the state to the nation and the nations of the earth—each of us has had a new book placed in our hands. Wherever we find ourselves, our new book has been tailor-made for us. Each and every step we take inscribes a flow of new words on the blank pages. The words tell about God and His presence with us, which will enable us to see this era through. Whether with our lives or with our pens or both, we are writing our books to and for Him. Our response is precious to Him:

Then those who feared the Lord talked often one to another; and the Lord listened and heard it, and a book of remembrance was written before Him of those who reverenced and worshipfully feared the Lord and who thought on His name.

And they shall be Mine, says the Lord of hosts, in that day when I publicly recognize and openly declare them to be My jewels (My special possession, My peculiar treasure). And I will spare them, as a man spares his own son who serves him.

MALACHI 3:16–17, AMP

Every past experience—good and bad, easy and difficult, triumphant and defeating, lucrative and impoverishing—each has prepared you to write this book. Your personality, your family, every bit of your uniqueness will craft a new piece of art, a book that will speak of the majesty and awesomeness of God.

It is time to pick up your book, so to speak, and begin to write!

4

Change, Whether You Like It or Not

My MOTHER DIED when I was young. I was a freshman in college, still a teenager.

Suddenly my family unit ceased to exist. The closest relationship I had ever had just vanished. Roles changed. Nothing was normal. Family mealtimes were devoid of pleasure. All my father could cook was grilled steak and fried eggs, and I was no help because I did not want to spend time in my mother's kitchen. Family members moved through the days with empty eyes and grief-gutted hearts.

With my mother's death, my hope vanished. Because hope was gone, faith faltered. I was numb, robotically going through the motions of daily life. I felt as if I had to wade through quicksand just to make it to bedtime. Then came the endless nights, when my thoughts raced faster than the Daytona 500, my feelings raged like terrible storms and fear crouched ready to overtake me. Fear of what?

Of everything—the future, relationships, significance, belonging, fear that I would even make it.

Then, within the first month after my mother's death, both of my paternal grandparents died, as well. My world just fell apart. I constantly thought, *This cannot be happening!* I was too young to deal with it. For a long time I was at a loss. I did not know what to think or what to say or how to act. I would go somewhere with my friends and feel totally disconnected from them. I could be in a room filled with people and feel as though a Plexiglas partition was dividing me from the others. I could see them and they could see me, but we could not touch each other. They lived in a world I was no longer part of—a world of family, security, love, connectedness and happiness.

Too quickly, I had discovered just how uncertain life really is. Now I knew that death was only a heartbeat away. In my isolation, I felt weird. I no longer saw things the way my friends did. Something inside of me had died. I had lost my mooring point. My future seemed bleak, and my mind was filled with overwhelming sadness. I had very little desire to go on living, and no goals except to make it through each day.

I kept going through the motions of attending classes, eating meals, going to bed at night. I even dated and went on a few exciting adventures like swimming in the flooded Missouri River. Yet the whole time, I was empty inside, devoid of any sense of connectedness to other people or to our mutual activities. This went on endlessly as I trudged through the sludge of life.

To this day, I am not really sure how I got through that time. I certainly did not have the life skills to work through it. No one except my college academic counselor and the school nurse seemed to know what to do with me. And they barely knew. I ended up in intensive coaching with a Christian psychiatrist as I went about recovering, regrouping and rebuilding my life. I had to relearn who

I was and what my reality consisted of. I had to relearn how to live in a healthy way.

After several years, I began to come out of the despair and hopelessness. I began to feel again. With my returned feelings came the sense that maybe I had a future ahead of me after all. Tenuously, I began to dream again about the future. Yet even in my dreaming, questions crept around in the back of my mind: *Will I ever get past this sense of being in never-never land? Will I have to keep going around this hamster wheel of struggling with past thoughts and ongoing fears? Will I start over, only to lose again? How can I be sure that what I plan will work out?*

I knew the Bible, but I could not connect to it. I knew it said that the foundation of the Lord stands sure, but those were only words. I would grab moments of exhilaration about the future, only to sink into despair because something had happened that reinforced my worst fear. Then there were the times when I thought I was ready to move forward, and nothing would budge. I felt like a plane in a holding pattern, unable to land. The future seemed to dissipate before me like fog.

Upheaval and Shaking

Jeremiah knew about times of turmoil and devastation. And he also knew that God was in charge. " '[The people of the land] will fight against you, but they shall not prevail against you. For I am with you,' says the LORD, 'to deliver you' " (Jeremiah 1:19). Jeremiah knew that things would have to be rooted out, pulled down and destroyed before the words of God could come to pass (see Jeremiah 1:10).

I read about an earthquake that struck off the island of Tonga in the Pacific Ocean early in 2009. It shook an erupting underwater volcano, which raised fears of increased lava and ash flows. "In the short term it is very damaging and will have limited, localized effects," a scientist said, because the ash could kill coral reefs and marine animals. "But an underwater explosion is really a wonderful thing, because it's creating new land. This kind of activity helps develop reef systems and helps preserve marine life."[1]

I thought that this was a remarkable statement—that a seeming disaster really can be a good thing in the long run. The scientist saw the earthquake and volcano through a different lens than most; he could see beyond the immediate emergency. He could see the potential for good.

Why do I mention this? Because when something new begins to emerge, the first thing you and I will usually notice is the shaking, uprooting, dismantling, wrenching removal of what used to be there. When God gets ready to do a new thing, He first removes whatever part of the old thing remains that may withstand the new. Often, that includes our defenses. People resist change. We resist new things until they overpower us. We seldom remember that a time of rebuilding and replanting is guaranteed to come right after a time of destruction.

Behind every seeming disaster, God is doing the ultimate new thing—He is bringing His Kingdom to earth. He is creating a Church that can move into a Kingdom mentality. He is drawing men and women to Himself, even though they do not always know why He is allowing them to go through such hard times.

This process of God is not new. Each time He initiates a new season, He brings a fresh emphasis on something that has become lost in the "stuff" of life. He knows that His Church people tend to shrink-wrap and diminish what they know of the Kingdom and to adopt mindsets antithetical to His original intent—so He shakes things up. He does it in order to bring in fresh life.

In fact, one of the ways we can figure out what new thing God is doing is to ask, "What is fresh?" In Isaiah 42:9, the Hebrew word *chadash* can be translated either as "new" or "fresh."[2] "Behold, the former things have come to pass, and *new* [fresh] things I declare; before they spring forth I tell you of them" (emphasis added). The essence of something new is freshness, something that has life and vitality, something that is not wilted or brown around the edges.

Who, What, When, Where, How

To spot God's new move and align ourselves with it, we need to make ourselves think in fresh and different ways. To think in a different way, we must evaluate ourselves, as I mentioned in the previous chapter. We need to consider our generational frame of reference, our personal modes of expression and our personal history. We need to make simple changes, even as simple as swapping out part of our daily routine.

Think about these questions as you look toward the new: What have you done in the past, and with whom did you do it? Did it succeed? Is it an ongoing activity or role? If you change what you are doing, the people you are doing it with, when you are doing it, where you are doing it or how you are doing it, you may find yourself in a whole new place.

Let me give an example from our church. For several years as part of our school of equipping, we have taught a class about how to study the Bible. For the first few years, the class was held on Thursday evenings. A big class was ten people, and I am not sure we ever had that many. A few months ago, we moved it to Sunday mornings. Sixty people showed up. We also changed the way we taught it. Instead of having one teacher, we implemented a team of teachers. This resulted in a much shorter lecture time and an intentional break-out time for small discussion groups. The whole thing became fresh, and God blessed it.

To explore different ways of thinking and doing things, we must keep exposing ourselves to new books, new ideas, new people, new groups, new methods and new options. Speaking of new people, we should ask ourselves, *With whom have I surrounded myself? Are these people willing to move with me into something new?* Sometimes we need to reach across streams and camps in the Body of Christ and break out of our self-limiting labels.

What Is Different This Time?

In this new era, you must be willing to do things differently at every turn. You must develop flexibility and agility; they will keep you childlike—and fresh. As you move through this next season of your life, you can then expect to bring others with you into the new—if you remember that what worked in the last season will not necessarily work in this one.

Overhead projectors still work, for example, but if you use one today, what message are you communicating to an iPod generation? If you have decided to move beyond the church building and into the marketplace, what does that mean? And are you willing to give up yesterday's pet project for something that God is emphasizing today?

How do you think in terms of money? Nationally and globally, we are moving into a very different economic environment. Will you continue to pay for goods and services with money, or sometimes by bartering instead? How will you manage if your 401(k) investments fail?

What is your point of reference or support structure? Will that need to change? For instance, the primary structure of reference for a stay-at-home mom will be her immediate family; for a student, it will be a friendship network; for an employee or employer, it will be the workplace. Whatever your reference point, changes are on the doorstep in this new time.

Changes All Over

No category of life is exempt from this current time of massive change. Let's take a look at a number of specific areas.

Religious Scene

We find that we are living in an increasingly secularized culture. The Church is no longer the centering influence in society. When I was growing up, most people went to church. Family life centered on home and church. Not that the local church was necessarily filled with life—yet it was a bastion of goodness and morality. Everyone participated. Not anymore.

At the same time as people are dropping out of church life, a plethora of "foreign" religions are appearing in every city. This is partially because the United States is such a melting pot for other nationalities. Other religions are imported, demystified and popularized by the media. Americans have adopted a tolerance for other expressions of faith, and the broad range of choices we now see has become disorienting.

Furthermore, even believers who have stayed in Christian churches, including Spirit-filled churches, seem to be suffering from disenchantment and agitation. Even in my own church, I am aware of an undercurrent of disenchantment with the status quo. We are hungry for more, for a fresh expression of the Spirit's power and presence in the Church. As a result, while people are drawing back from formal legalism and traditions that do not convey true life, churches are emerging that are life-giving and transforming.

Political Scene

Our national political scene has also changed. Here in America, we are sitting in a political cauldron. Power has shifted, and national leaders lean far to the left, embracing abortion, same-sex marriage, embryonic stem cell research and socialistic inclinations. Politics have become more and more polarized, and verbal wars break out over almost every issue. It seems that both sides in every argument have become increasingly vitriolic.

We now have an African-American president, yet an underlying racial division plagues the nation at large. Immigration issues, military decisions, the environment . . . through it all, righteousness and justice are rare commodities. Corruption, bribery and scandals proliferate. Few really care for the poor.

How should the Gospel of the Kingdom affect our political thinking? What should we pray for? How should we participate in the political process?

My prayer for both America and other nations in the world is that the political wars will provoke an emergence of people who will, as the prophet Micah wrote, be committed "to do justly, to love mercy, and to walk humbly with [their] God" (Micah 6:8). Along with others, I have been calling forth a new spirit within our Senate and House of Representatives, the White House and the Cabinet, a wave of awakening to God in the least expected places. I want to see angelic hosts begin to do God's bidding in high places. I want to see them go behind closed doors and awaken the hearts of dead men and women to the realities of their salvation. I want to hear about politicians experiencing dreams and sovereign encounters with the living God. I want to see them begin to know that there is a God who is bigger than any heads of nations—One who can turn nations with one flick of His finger and one breath from His nostril.

Geophysical Crises

Almost daily, the news carries stories about new natural disasters—a flood, an earthquake, a mudslide, an ice storm, a hurricane. No climate or region of the world seems exempt. These geophysical crises affect people across all socioeconomic lines, although the repercussions fall hardest on the poor. Consider Haiti and the 2010 earthquake there.

The challenge here is to know what God wants each of us to do in such times. Should we shore up in particular areas of preparedness? Should we stock up on vital supplies ahead of time, stay alert and be ready for anything? How can we best help in times of emergency? Is God trying to say something here?

Economic Shaking

For some time, we Americans have been riding on the edge of economic devastation. The subprime mortgage crisis and credit shutdown pummeled the stock markets of the world and paralyzed both large and small businesses. Corporate greed has been uncovered at grievous levels, and all of us suffer for it.

In my country, will recession descend into depression? Will unemployment ever decline? Will spending and saving ever be the same again? Where once we took so much for granted, now we ask ourselves, *Will I have a house, money, a car, clothes, food to feed my family, gas to get to work—a job? Will I be broke? What is God saying to me in this uncertain economic time?*

Unshakable Kingdom

In every sphere of human activity, God is saying, "I am the only One who will not change." He is the Everlasting Rock, and He cannot be shaken by any religious, political, geophysical or economic crisis. He is not trembling with dismay. He knows what is coming next. He invites each and every person into an authentic and simple relationship with Jesus, in whom "we live and move and have our being" (Acts 17:28, NIV).

All of the changes around us, whether we welcome them or not, point us to God. "Therefore, since we are receiving a kingdom which cannot be shaken, let us have grace, by which we may serve God acceptably with reverence and godly fear" (Hebrews 12:28).

We seem to have forgotten the basic truths about God. In his article "What's Wrong with Our Gospel?"[3] Frank Viola lists three truths in particular that he feels Christians need to regain in order to meet the days ahead. One truth is simply the *reality of the indwelling Christ*. We are called to live not by our own strength, but through the life of Jesus Christ within us. Paul said that one of the great mysteries of the faith is "Christ in you, the hope of glory" (Colossians 1:27). Paul also said, "I am crucified with Christ: nevertheless I live; yet not I, but Christ liveth in me: and the life which I now live in the flesh I live by the faith of the Son of God, who loved me, and gave himself for me" (Galatians 2:20, KJV). Jesus said that His life came from the life of the Father living within Him, and that we are supposed to live by His life in and with us (see John 14:9–11). We do not live *for* Christ, we live *in* and *through* Him.

Second, Viola says that we have lost our sense of the *greatness of Christ*. I often think about the religious pictures we put up on our walls. Often, they portray Jesus as our Helper. But He is so much more than that. He existed before the foundation of the world. Through Him the worlds were created. He has always been, and He always will be. He is the Alpha and Omega, the beginning and the end. He is the Captain of the Hosts, portrayed in the book of Revelation as riding a great white horse. He is the ruling, reigning King, the King of kings and Lord of lords.

Third, Viola says we have lost sight of *God's eternal purpose*. The Father designed human beings as co-participants with Him. His Genesis 1:28 mandate tells us, "Then God blessed them, and God said to them, 'Be fruitful and multiply; fill the earth and subdue it; have dominion over the fish of the sea, over the birds of the air, and over every living thing that moves on the earth.'" God's eternal purpose began before the Fall. He sent Jesus so that we could return to His Kingdom mandate. We have lost sight of it so completely that it strikes us as a new idea.

What a novelty—to be created in God's image, to be His image-bearers in the world, to transmit His will to every part of the created world! A good part of the "new" that we seek in this time centers on our restoration to the position God designed us for in the first place—that in Him and through Him, we steward the little piece of the planet where He has situated us. Having been renewed by Him, we do not undertake our stewardship out of duty, but instead out of a relationship of healthy love.

Jesus loved what His Father loved and hated what His Father hated. His whole life revolved around His Father. That is what the Father wants for each of us. In all of our striving and reaching toward the "new," let's be sure to return to the core of biblical truth: Christ in us, the hope of glory!

5

What Are You Changing To?

YEARS AGO, I began to consider writing a book. However, I did not know how to do it. I had written papers for school, as well as articles for magazines. I had created notes from which to preach sermons. However, I had never written a whole book. It seemed like a formidable task. I wondered, *How do people write that much? How do they come up with an idea worth writing about? How do they figure out how to compose it? How do they find the time?*

Furthermore, I knew I would need a computer in order to write a book, but I had no clue how to make use of a computer. It was inevitable that I would have to replace my old typewriter, and I could not expect a secretary to handle all my word processing needs. *Word processing?* Yes, in addition to the challenge of producing thousands of words that could communicate something people would want to read, I would also have to change my vocabulary.

From now on, *typing* would be called *keyboarding* and *writing* would be called *word processing*. And to accomplish any of this, I needed to get up to speed on a daunting new piece of equipment called a computer.

I bought an Apple Macintosh computer with 256K RAM and set about learning how to use it. Every time I took a misstep, this picture of a bomb would appear on the screen. Knowing nothing about computers and how they operate, I thought the thing was about to blow up. That shows you how clueless I was. Everything was new to me.

Eventually, my skills improved. Today, I cannot imagine living without a computer. I could never have guessed that I would some-day carry a laptop with me wherever I went. Even more amazing, my iPhone has become a much more versatile device than my old telephone and laptop put together!

Change Leads Somewhere

The wrenching changes occurring all around us today are difficult at times, but they are taking us somewhere. Change leads to something new. Any new thing usually seems intimidating at first. But as any of us who are old enough to predate personal computers can testify, the learning curve involved in facing the new is definitely worth tackling.

I remember the first time I went overseas to minister. I had spent most of my time in the United States and Canada, where everybody spoke English and where people were pretty much like me. On that first overseas ministry trip, my hosts could speak English, but my audience could not, so I had to preach with an interpreter. Although I tried to pack for the climate and culture, some of my clothing was far from suitable. I soon realized that my mode of expression was way too American. I kept running into customs that were new to me, not to mention unfamiliar foods. For days, it seemed as if I had to figure out everything from scratch, even the most basic things.

With everything so new and strange, I discovered a new problem, one that I could not have anticipated. I was used to connecting with people who were like me, so I used stories that assumed a certain familiarity with the world as I knew it. But overseas, everything was so different. I thought, *I don't know these people at all. I cannot talk with most of them because I don't know their language. I have no idea what they do for a living or what their family life is like. I don't know how they think and feel. How can I know what they need? How can I minister to them?*

Although people looked different from me and talked differently, ate different food and followed different customs, they were still human beings who struggled with life issues. It did not take me long to realize that people everywhere have the same personal struggles. We shared the same God, and God's truth transcends cultural differences.

Once I learned how other people thought and felt and what their life experience was like, and once I identified the ways in which they were the *same* as me, I no longer felt like a stranger. Now I could accommodate who I was to what they needed. I could keep learning more about them, and I could continue to move into my new role in a different culture. Each time I would minister overseas in new places, I had to come up with a new set of ministry skills, and yet the whole process of adjustment and change would always lead me—and the ones to whom I ministered—to new levels of purpose and fulfillment.

Trying New Things

A while ago, I started to realize that something had died in my church. The freshness of the Holy Spirit had gone stale. Everything seemed like a well-worn formality, routine and lifeless. What had happened? Had we missed God? Had He bypassed us and gone somewhere else? Clearly something needed to change. But what? What could the fresh direction possibly look like? How would I recognize it?

Then one ordinary Sunday, something very simple happened. I was talking about banners from a scriptural standpoint. For the purpose of illustration, I asked one of our men to pick up one of the large silk banners we had on hand at the edge of the sanctuary, and I told him to walk back and forth with it. As soon as he did, I began to notice something unusual. It seemed as though wherever he took the banner, it stirred up spiritual life and activity in the people he passed.

Immediately, I took things a step further. I did something new. I put aside the rest of my sermon, and I asked the people in the congregation to pick out a banner and begin to wave them back and forth. That was so simple, and yet it ushered in a new wave of the Holy Spirit's presence. The more we waved the banners, the greater the presence of the Holy Spirit became. We had some of the Life back!

In the next few weeks, the women who made the banners produced more of them, and we filled the sanctuary with people waving banners. Now the Holy Spirit began to return in full force. All we had needed was to do something new!

When something is genuinely new, it can bring the freshness back into our lives. Once again we get excited, and we feel invigorated, energized, passionate. Something ignites in our hearts. We are fired up. Especially when the new thing is something that God is doing, our new experiences bring life back, when only a short time before we were desperately searching for it, trying to satisfy our gnawing spiritual hunger and endeavoring to catch the wind of the Spirit again.

Seizing the Initiative

The same thing happened when Joshua became the leader of the Israelites after Moses died. Suddenly, everything was new. Moses had led the children of Israel into phenomenal new freedom from Egypt, but the newness wore off almost immediately. Their wilderness wandering ended up lasting an entire generation, and it got really "old." When Joshua inherited Moses' leadership role, most of the people had never seen Egypt because they had been born and raised in tents during this long, transitional wilderness time.

The promises of God to the Israelites were still awaiting fulfillment. Now it was up to Joshua to start a new campaign. Abruptly, the people's complaints and the bitterness of their deferred hope were broken off because they were on the move, advancing into the promised territory at last. It was time.

New land! A fresh mandate. This would require new attitudes and skills. New courage and confidence overtook the people. This was their new day. No longer would they only talk about doing things—now they were beginning to actually do them! They were advancing. Canaan was within sight. Within a few days, they began to conquer the land that had seemed unassailable before.

As soon as the first piece of the borderland was taken, excitement and expectation created a new surge of momentum. Like a car refueled to get back in the race, the people's army of Israel moved with increasing effectiveness. Mountains and valleys fell before their advance. Fortified cities became theirs. They ended up deep inside the land of promise, where they had never been before. Suddenly, these descendants of former slaves who had grown up as desert wanderers became full landowners. Each one of them could possess a portion of Canaan. Caleb shouted out, "Give me my mountain!" and he got it. His daughter said, "Give me the upper and lower springs!" and they were hers.

Caleb had waited 45 years for this day. He was 85 years old. Joshua himself was about 100 years old. Now that the time had come, new energy surged through their elderly bodies. Their long wait was over. Their desperation was rewarded. Their faithfulness had paid off. Victory was now assured:

> Then the children of Judah came to Joshua in Gilgal. And Caleb the son of Jephunneh the Kenizzite said to him: "You know the word which the LORD said to Moses the man of God concerning you and me in Kadesh Barnea. I was forty years old when Moses the servant of the LORD sent me from Kadesh Barnea to spy out the land, and I brought back word to him as it was in my heart. Nevertheless my brethren who went up with me made the heart of the people melt, but I wholly followed the LORD my GOD. So Moses swore on that day, saying, 'Surely the land where your foot has trodden shall be your inheritance and your children's forever, because you have wholly followed the LORD my GOD.' And now, behold, the LORD has kept me alive, as He said, these forty-five years, ever since the LORD spoke this word to Moses while Israel wandered in the wilderness; and now, here I am this day, eighty-five years old. As yet I am as strong this day as on the day that Moses sent me; just as my strength was then, so now is my strength for war, both for going out and for coming in. Now therefore, give me this mountain of which the LORD spoke in that day; for you heard in that day how the Anakim were there, and that the cities were great and fortified. It may be that the LORD will be with me, and I shall be able to drive them out as the LORD said."
>
> And Joshua blessed him, and gave Hebron to Caleb the son of Jephunneh as an inheritance.
>
> *JOSHUA 14:6–13*

What is your mountain? What is mine? What new and fresh territory has God led us to conquer? Is it time? Is our long wilderness trek over?

The Birth of the New

When a baby is born, excitement is the word of the day. Any woman who has ever had a baby or anyone who has ever watched a birth knows what I am talking about, especially if they remember the first time they experienced it. Look at that tiny person! Little fingers and toes, perfect little nose, amazing grunts and noises. All you can do is cry with joy and awe. It is one of the few things that makes a man cry.

And the birth is just the beginning. Before long, that baby begins to smile and look at the world with wide eyes. Within a year, that former newborn is almost a toddler, moving around and trying to put everything into his or her mouth. Those ten busy fingers never stop wiggling. This new little person is very much alive and growing.

Every new thing goes through a period of gestation, followed by a birth—and the birth is just the beginning. The new thing keeps getting renewed; it keeps growing and changing. Just as with a child, you cannot rewind and backtrack. You need to nurture the new thing even as you scramble to keep up with it. You did not realize this would require so much energy for so long.

Some of us hesitate before we commit ourselves to something new. For too many of us, traumas have laid down a foundation of debris-like baggage that can keep us from moving into the next new thing with youthful excitement. We may need renewing, cleaning up, rebuilding and repairing before we can participate. This can apply to individuals and to groups of people. God places the new wine of His Spirit into freshly rebuilt vessels.

Many people in the church world are coming out of a difficult season. They must be renewed and repaired after going through the wilderness of personal and corporate challenges. Some have faced family breakdowns, terminal diseases or health challenges; others have experienced job losses, economic disasters or internal paradigm shifts that created confusion and disequilibrium. The prevailing uncertainty in contemporary life has drained them. They need healing from the anger and bitterness, the hurt and rejection, the depression and guilt, the sense of powerlessness and emotional paralysis that result from painful and challenging experiences.

However, when I talk about moving into the new, I mean far more than merely being renewed following a traumatic experience. I am convinced that God is doing something fresh in the world today, not just in my corner of it or in a few special spots, but everywhere. It is bigger than the Israelites overtaking the Promised Land. It is global. We are entering a new era, and I am quite sure that we will need more retooling along the way.

We will receive part of what we need simply from recognizing that we are entering a time of newness. Energy comes from the renewed hopefulness and collaboration with other like-minded people. Anything that is new has come into being only a short time ago; it is a recent development. It is fresh, like a new coat of paint. When we acquire something new, like a new car or a new item of clothing, we enjoy both the improved capabilities and the novelty of using it. We like to discover more about it, even if it means conquering unknown territory. In other words, the very fact that we have only recently become aware of a new thing gives us an advantage in overcoming our unfamiliarity with it.

People define newness differently, depending on their age and experience. To those who are relatively young, everything seems new. For others, a new thing will seem more like a new expression, a new emphasis, a new way of seeing or doing an old thing, a new perspective. To them, a new thing will not be *all* new, but something about it will be fresh, involving a new thrust or a new mandate. It will require new skills or capacities, new ways of relating and new relationships.

What Does the Word *New* Mean?

The word *new* works. It sells things. Advertisers use it all the time. Of course, often the word communicates very little real information. Only insiders know what "New!" means in a given context.

People use *new* to mean something that has been changed or exchanged for the better, something that may have been recently discovered or something additional, such as new sources of energy. They mean something that has recently arrived or that has recently been established in a place, such as new neighbors. Moviegoers flock to see the latest new movie, even though the word *new* does little to describe the experience of watching it. A new edition is the latest in a sequence, the very most up-to-date and revised version.

New can also mean something unaccustomed or something people are inexperienced with, such as a new rule or a new job. We all know what it is like to navigate new applications of technology or new relationships, not to mention the broader "new global realities" we hear about on the news.

New can be used as an adjective for something tiny, as well as for something massive. New can be something you hold in your hand or something invisible and intangible. On your new, palm-sized iPod or iPhone, you can begin to learn a new-to-you language that will open to you new opportunities in a nation you have not yet visited.

Biblically, what does the word *new* mean, especially when applied to a move of God? New is used often in Scripture. In the Old Testament, God said to Isaiah,

> Behold, I will do a new thing,
> Now it shall spring forth;
> Shall you not know it?

> I will even make a road in the wilderness
> And rivers in the desert.

ISAIAH 43:19

The previous chapter in the book of Isaiah contains this well-known line: "Behold, the former things have come to pass, and *new* things I declare; before they spring forth I tell you of them" (Isaiah 42:9, emphasis added). These usages imply that God is replacing something that has already existed with something that is so completely refurbished that it seems all new.

In the book of Psalms, the word *new* is most often used with the word *song*, as in "sing to the LORD a new song" (Psalm 96:1; 98:1; 149:1; see also Psalm 33:3; 40:3; 144:9.)

In both the Old and the New Testaments, the word *new* is often coupled with the word *wine*. New wine is that which has been freshly made. As Jesus reminded us in one of His illustrations, new wine must be stored in new bottles (made in those days from animal skins) in order to be usable. In the same way, He pointed out, the new wine of the Holy Spirit can only be poured into renewed human spirits, lest it be squandered:

> No one sews a patch of unshrunk cloth on an old garment. If he does, the new piece will pull away from the old, making the tear worse. And no one pours new wine into old wineskins. If he does, the wine will burst the skins, and both the wine and the wineskins will be ruined. No, he pours new wine into new wineskins.

MARK 2:21–22, NIV

The people in those days used to rub oil into aged wineskins, regenerating them for reuse. They seldom made brand-new wineskins or wine bottles because they had renewed the previously used ones. In the same way, the sparkling new wine of the Spirit is poured into the newly anointed vessels of our renewed human spirits.

A New Awakening

In terms of the Kingdom of God, we are on the verge of a new great awakening, a revival of unprecedented proportions, a time when God's presence will fill His people in such an all-encompassing way that what we once thought was "the glory" will seem pale by comparison. William Seymour, the leader and visionary of the Azusa Street revival, prophesied in 1909 that another, greater move of God would occur about one hundred years in the future. His prophecy puts that new move of God right in our present time frame. With predictions such as this, we should not be surprised to see this time of shake-up and change coming upon the world and the Church like a conquering army.

That brings to mind a powerful experience I had a few years ago. I was scheduled to speak at a conference, and during the worship segment of one service, an unusual presence of God began to settle on me, carrying me into a vision that was like being in an IMAX 3D action movie.

In the vision, I saw a large number of men running toward me with weapons. They were muscular, battle-hardened and clothed in animal skins like rugged men of ancient times. In their hands were swords, clubs, axes, bows and shields. Some of them were on horses. Like the army in the movie *Braveheart*, they rushed toward me in attack mode. They were so aggressive and intimidating that I exclaimed to the Lord, "Are they for us or against us?"

He answered, "They are for you."

As soon as He uttered those words, it was as if I were taken up into the sky to the altitude where jets fly. It was night. I looked down at the United States, and I could see very few lights shining anywhere in the nation. The occasional lights were far removed from each other. I seemed to be flying over a whole continent that was scarcely inhabited, like a vast wilderness or at least a rural countryside.

However, the army I had seen started galloping across the

landscape, and as it did, lights began to turn on. Wherever the army passed through, lights began to appear, and they remained on after the army went by. The lights increased in number until the cities and towns across the nation—wherever people dwelt—were completely lit up. The lights became continuous in a huge swath; it looked as if a massive fire had been set on one coast and it had spread across to the other side of the continental United States, burning brightly.

Zooming in to Earth again, I saw that nothing deterred this galloping army. They were running right through walls, buildings, fences, mountains and all other obstacles. Skyscrapers, houses and billboards flew every which way as they hurtled right through them. Nothing slowed the men down. Clearly, this was a supernatural army. Not only were they more powerful than any human army, they were more courageous. They never hesitated. It was as if God had put a computer chip in them that gave them only one command: "Straight ahead. Never stop. Do not look back until you have reached the other side of the nation."

And the Lord said to me, simply, "This is My army."

At the time, I interpreted the vision as predictive of a spiritual army from heaven that would sweep across the nation. What I did not grasp was the significance of the destruction it left in its wake. As current events have unfolded both nationally and globally, both inside and outside the Church, such destruction has begun. Now I can see the implication of the leveling of entire organizations, as well as the destruction of long-established structures, corporations, governments, churches and so on. Some of these things are not corrupt or evil in the commonly thought-of way; they are simply missing the mark in a time when God is increasingly serious about who we are and how we do things. Whatever is in the path of the divine army, anything dark or not aligned with God's purposes or character, is being flung down and set on fire for both destruction and illumination.

God is doing something brand new, and He wants to fill the darkness with His light. Before He can come in the all-encompassing manner in which He wants to come, certain things must be moved out of the way. Nothing is God-resistant. God is removing His blessing from agendas and organizations large and small. On a personal level as well as a corporate level, He is shaking things up. He wants to bring in His Kingdom, to the point that He is essentially throwing "grenades" into programs and activities that preoccupy people's attention. He Himself wants to do a new thing in the earth—to remove distractions so that people will turn to their number-one priority—God Himself.

He is in the middle of breaking our trust in everything that neuters our faith in Him. He is looking for a people who are radically surrendered to Him and dependent on Him. He must have people who will risk all for the sake of the advance of His Kingdom.

We do not need to feel anxious when we see the falling apart of so much that once seemed immutable to change. It is happening whether or not we prayed for it or expected it, and I believe God is orchestrating the destruction for multiple purposes:

- To cleanse our trust by removing whatever keeps us from leaning wholly on Him.
- To break down formal structures that impede the coming of His Kingdom so that the original intent of Pentecost as a grassroots, bottom-up movement (as opposed to a hierarchical, structured institution) can be regained.
- To move out of the way whatever consumes our time, energy and devotion—anything that is no longer part of our assignment.
- To restore our focus on relationships instead of tasks. Relationships—first with God and then with people—should frame the mandate for our tasks.

- To create desperation. When everything we have trusted in breaks down or goes away, we cry out to God. This crying out brings help in the form of salvation and deliverance, and it carries us into a new place.

Can you hear the heavenly army thundering across the land? Have they galloped through your own life, your church or your locality?

Begin to lift up your voice and cry out to God in honest desperation. Allow His cry to fill your mouth, knowing that His purpose is not destruction, it is reformation. This is the cry that God hears.

Desperately Uncertain

ONE THING I KNOW—nothing is certain. We are fooling ourselves if we think so.

All we have to do is look at the daily news, filled with disasters large and small. Recall the tsunami that devastated Asia in 2004. No one expected it. No one was prepared for it. That part of the world will never be the same. More recently, think about the 2010 earthquake in Haiti. No one expected an earthquake in Haiti, even though a known fault line runs under Port-au-Prince. It had not been active for two hundred years. Yet with no warning, the whole city was wracked with devastation, and the aftershocks—physical, economic, psychological—will continue for generations.

I know of a couple who had dedicated their lives to working in Haiti. They had just finished a new church building that could seat two thousand people, and they were purchasing seats for the sanctuary and preparing for the dedication. When the earthquake hit, in one moment their life's work crashed into rubble.

In Jeremiah 29, God told Jeremiah and the exiles from Israel to go ahead and marry, have children, build houses and plant gardens. At the time, they had been taken into captivity and exiled in Babylon. Their future was not theirs to control. Yet God was telling them to make plans, live well and build a future. Regardless of their uncertain status as exiles, they were to move ahead—in fact, to flourish:

> For I know the thoughts that I think toward you, says the LORD, thoughts of peace and not of evil, to give you a future and a hope. Then you will call upon Me and go and pray to Me, and I will listen to you. And you will seek Me and find Me, when you search for Me with all your heart. I will be found by you, says the LORD.
>
> *JEREMIAH 29:11–14*

Temporal uncertainty is part of the plan of the unchanging God of the universe. It helps us let go of the past and become willing to move into the future.

The Exodus

Let's backtrack to the story of the people of Israel in Moses' time. What happened just prior to their exodus from Egypt (see Exodus 7–11) and then in the ensuing forty years in the wilderness can help us understand the events of the twenty-first century.

First, we need to get past our overromanticized version of the story. We usually read through those ten horrific plagues in Egypt in fast succession. Some people can even make them sound entertaining. Plague after plague, the great escape, the Red Sea ... and we already know the end of the story, so we really do not think about what it must have seemed like to the people of Israel at the time. They did not know the future, not even Moses. Moses' knowledge consisted of only what he had been told by God's voice. For the most part, he was operating in the dark like everyone else.

Have you ever thought about the level of uncertainty the Israelites endured? This time of the plagues was a massive, unexpected shake-up. What was going on? One disaster outdid the previous one. The world was falling apart. If you had been an ordinary Hebrew man or woman living in a humble dwelling, toiling away day after day under the hot sun for your Egyptian masters, what would you make of the situation? One sunny morning, an alarming thing happens: Those who have gone earliest to the river to draw water for their masters are streaming back in distress, with empty buckets—or with their water buckets stained red. The Nile has turned to *blood*. All the fish are dead. No one can comprehend it, and it affects everyone. This is serious.

About the time you and your fellow slaves have rallied to figure out what to do, the river water returns to normal. What was that all about? But wait, now what are all these *frogs* doing underfoot? Every place you put your hand or foot in your master's house, there is another one. Is this a nightmare? Where did they come from—the bloody river water? What is going on?

Next thing you know, the frogs die off en masse. As you rake them into stinking piles, *flies* start swarming not only on the piles, but on every square inch of everything. You cannot even open your mouth to exclaim about them for fear of swallowing one. Has all of hell opened up?

The people of Israel did not have a clue what was happening. This was long before cell phones, TV, radio, CNN, the Internet and Twitter. Nobody was reporting live on the conversations between Moses, Aaron and Pharaoh. We are talking about two million to three million people who did not see the big picture behind these events. As those ten plagues overtook Egypt, the Hebrew slaves were subjected to the suffering almost as much as the Egyptians. Even though the Hebrews' livestock did not die of disease, they themselves did not break out in boils and their firstborn did not die, yet they could see and smell death and disaster all around as they worked for their masters.

To say the least, the people of Israel must have felt very uncertain. Rocked this way and that by one thing after another, all they knew for sure was that nothing was normal anymore. It was beginning to look like it would never end. Even when the Israelites started to catch on (see Exodus 12), I am sure that most of them understood only a little of what God was doing. They were thrilled when they were instructed to plunder their wealthier Egyptian neighbors, and even more thrilled when their neighbors complied by loading them down with valuables. They were obedient when they were told to prepare for a mass exodus. But what did they know, really? Did it make any sense to put lamb's blood on the lintel and doorposts? Did this never-ending cascade of disruptive events and unusual instructions fill their hearts with peace and confidence and joyful anticipation? I doubt it.

The people of Israel were far from comfortable. The time they were in was traumatic—threats and disasters piled up relentlessly, and all they could do was try to keep up. On both the individual and corporate levels, the disruptive events going on were affecting everyone, just as the things going on in our time do. And like us, most of them probably defaulted to a myopic view of their difficult situation. Sometimes all people can see in such times is the uncertainty in their own homes, their communities, their work or their spiritual families.

In trying times, we often cannot handle it when we start thinking about the bigger picture. We have our hands too full of our own troubles. *What is God up to?* we think. *Does He not care about my health, wealth and personal fulfillment?* Some of us in my country even ask, *Does He not realize that I am an American and that my life is supposed to be carefree?* As a people, Americans do not cope well with uncertainty. Most of us have not had much practice with radical change, readjustment and acceptance of pain. Unlike the Haitian people, we might reach for our wallets or pill bottles before we would consider worshiping God in the open street in front of where our church used to stand before the earthquake turned it into a pile of rubble.

God took Israel out of a system that they had known for over four hundred years. They were slaves, true, but at least they knew what to expect. Yet God knew what He was doing. Yes, there would be pain along the new way, not to mention uncertainty. But His pillars of cloud and fire would keep moving, and the people would realize that their other options had disappeared along with the Egyptian chariots in the Red Sea. No turning back, people. We are going somewhere you have never gone before, somewhere new. Canaan lies ahead. Welcome to the wilderness!

Little did they realize that the Kingdom was advancing.

What Now?

The Exodus shows us a picture of a new kingdom being brought out of an old system. In many ways, the same thing goes on with us. Massive conflict leads to extreme, prolonged, even overwhelming uncertainty, which leads to a cry of desperation, which may lead to more of the same—until the day, possibly years away, when we finally emerge into our new Kingdom reality. After enough pressure, the people of the Church can be brought into an identity that has the power to overcome.

The people of Israel did not develop their new identity while they were still in Egypt. They developed it in a new place, over time and through many difficulties. The people of Israel had to separate from their slave status in Egypt in the same way that the Church must be separated from the culture around it.

When we repeat the words, "Thy Kingdom come, Thy will be done, on earth as it is in heaven," what are we praying? Are we praying for a cleaned-up version of what we know already, or for something heavenly and new? When Israel left Egypt, their exodus represented the beginning of a huge paradigm shift for them. It is the same with us. What happened with the people of Israel happens with the family of God over and over as the Kingdom advances.

Right now, we are in the throes of a big advance. It may not feel too great, on a personal or a corporate level. We may be tempted to grumble before we think of crying out to God for relief—especially when we figure out that what He sends may not resemble our idea of "relief." (Manna, anyone? How about some quail?)

It is so easy to forget that He has everything under control, He never drops a beat, His eye is on the sparrow—and that His ways simply are not our ways. He is bringing in His Kingdom, and we happen to be part of the process.

The whole time, God is using what is on our plates to bring us to a new place. He wants to rattle our cages. In His love, He wants us to stop trusting in our own brilliant schemes and daily routines and turn to Him as never before. As more and more people cry out to Him in their personal lives, their voices will blend into a corporate outcry and merge into the cry God hears.

Then God Hits Pause

Sometimes moving into the new place God has for us is quite simple. Other times it is just the opposite. How difficult or challenging it is will depend on the magnitude of the change. Joseph had to make a huge shift when suddenly the Midianites purchased him and took him to Egypt. Betrayed by his brothers, sold into slavery and transported to a totally foreign place, he had to adjust to an unfamiliar culture, a drastic change in his status and much more. No longer a favorite son and (not so favorite) brother, he was now a slave in a strange land, alone. That was a big change.

Many changes for us have led up to the challenging economic season we are now in. Our military-industrial complex used to help maintain a significant measure of prosperity because it created and maintained an impressive number of jobs and built factories. Now, more than armory, artillery, planes, tanks and ships, we have sophisticated technology operated by an expertly trained intelligence corps who must adapt to meet the ever-shifting tactics of terrorists. So even the military is shifting away from industry to technology and information resources. That shift creates a large chasm for those people trained for industry, who are now ill equipped to function in this new age.

On a more mundane level, we became accustomed to the television-marketing partnership. Advertising on TV used to guarantee lucrative results. Now television advertising is going out of business as everyone transitions into Internet communications. Major networks are suffering because of diminishing viewing audiences. Companies do not want to put their money where their target audience has dwindled.

These are just a couple of changes in the world in which we live, and they parallel changes in the Church. More changes are piling up weekly, including changes in how we view ourselves as the Church and as individual Christians, how we accommodate to the changes in the world around us, how we determine strategies and goals and more. We are living in a time of great uncertainty. Many of us just plain do not know what to do or how to proceed. Our old methods no longer work. Without answers to the uncertainty, we feel paralyzed. Too often, we cannot discern what God is saying—or locate

Him at all. Sometimes, it is as if He has pushed a pause button, and we are stuck, frozen, incapable of resolving the situation.

As dependent on the wind of the Spirit as a sailboat, we find ourselves stranded, not moving. We do not know how long we will have to remain this way, although most of us understand that the more all-encompassing and far-reaching the uncertainty is, the longer it may take to move into something new. The larger the entity is, the slower it changes. If God is moving us into a whole new era of human life on earth, no wonder we feel confused.

Already, our losses are considerable, which can lead us to fear and despair—or to faith. We might as well accept that uncertainty is a fact of life. It is designed to propel us to search for meaning, forcing us into a new reality. As long as we keep trying to go back to the "good old days," or keep whining about how we miss the "flesh pots of Egypt" (see Exodus 16:3), we will remain unsettled, unsure, tenuous, even fearful. Lacking assurance, we may become suspicious and skeptical. With everything changeable, ambiguous, fitful, unsteady, unforeseeable and unpredictable, including our reactions, we do not know what or whom to trust.

Trauma Requires Healing

It is not too much to say that we have been traumatized. Our present uncertainty seems to point to an underlying traumatic event or series of events. A trauma is more than a simple wound; it is unexpected, severe wounding with peripheral damage, brutalizing to spirit, soul and body.

One afternoon I was praying about a particular situation I had been going through. I asked the Lord, "What is holding me back from moving forward?" And I heard Him say, "Trauma."

That sounded impressive to me. I understood physical trauma, and I knew about trauma centers. Trauma requires specialized attention. Evidently I needed to figure out what kind of attention mine would need. I had not been in an automobile accident or on a battlefield of war. I had not been in an earthquake, a tsunami or a fire. I had not witnessed any criminal brutality.

I had suffered some significant setbacks and losses. I had been disoriented by the strain of some relationships. The trauma of it (although I had not thought of it as trauma) affected my ability to cope. I experienced an uncharacteristic fatigue. At times I wanted to escape somehow and would sabotage myself with negative self-talk. While normally I am a sociable person, I wanted to withdraw into the safety of my own home.

I did not like what I was experiencing. I could see myself becoming indecisive. Some people get hostile, but that is rarely my nature. Worst of all, although I am a pastor, I struggled in connecting with God and people. God seemed far away, and I was sure that other people would not understand my dilemma.

I looked at what constitutes a trauma. I did some research online, and I learned that trauma contains three common elements:

1. Whatever had happened was unexpected.
2. The person was unprepared.
3. There was nothing they could do to keep it from happening.[1]

I also learned that trauma is not the same as stress. Trauma can be distinguished from stress by the following factors:

1. How quickly the upset is triggered
2. How frequently it is triggered
3. How intensely threatening the source of upset is
4. How long the upset lasts
5. How long it takes to calm down[2]

I discovered that whether an event causes trauma or not depends upon a host of factors, including:

1. The severity of the event
2. The individual's personal history
3. The larger meaning of the event to the individual
4. Coping skills as well as values and beliefs held by the individual
5. The reactions and support from family, friends and/or professionals[3]

Brain scans reveal that trauma actually changes the structure and function of the brain, affecting the cortex (center of thinking skills), the limbic system (center of emotions) and the brain stem (which controls basic survival skills). This is why trauma damage resists simple healing methods. Traumatized people often need not only emotional healing and/or deliverance, but also physical healing for their brains.

However, no healing can take place if people do not get down to the root of the issue and then make the necessary changes. Too many people, feeling (or being told by others) that they should just "get on with life," skip the restorative process. Resultantly, they cannot move into the future very well. They carry on with life, but they have been crippled by it. They limp along, just putting one foot in front of the other, hardly able to accept help from others even when it is offered. Overall, their confidence in themselves and in God rides on empty.

God told Isaiah, "In quietness and confidence shall be your strength" (Isaiah 30:15). Without confidence, strength dissipates. Fear moves into the house next door, displacing the hope that used to dwell there. New moves seem risky. Trust evaporates. "Fight or flight" reactions spring up.

Where can we find the healing we need? In the One who is

perfect love Himself, because His perfect love casts out all our fear (see 1 John 4:18) and heals us in every way. God Himself is the only one who can propel us past the impossibilities and into a new place of strength. We need a fresh encounter with God. He will enable us to see our future with hope. Some of this may come through a relationship where we are being coached by a trained professional.

Abraham and Sarah were overcome with a vision for the future when they met God (see Genesis 17–18). Jacob gained courage to face Esau, who represented his future, when he met God in that all-night wrestling match (see Genesis 32). Gideon could move beyond his hiding place in the winepress and onto the battlefield once God sent His angel to overtake his mind, defeat his fear and infuse him with hope (see Judges 6–7). Hosea's troubled wife found hope when God drew her into the wilderness alone. Her Valley of Achor (Trouble) became her door of hope (see Hosea 2:15). Stephen could face his imminent death with confidence because he communed with God (see Acts 6–7).

All of these people received supernatural enablement, so it is possible. All of these people found God in the middle of their greatest uncertainty, so that is possible, too.

Hope Is Expectation

When I lay hold of Jesus afresh (or He lays hold of me), I understand that the long wilderness of instability has been worth it. Hope is expectation, and that expectation for the future delivers me into it. God *will* save me. My desperation made me cry out to Him in spite of my fears, and now He will not let me down. Hope is my new reality:

> We who have fled [to Him] for refuge might have mighty indwelling strength and strong encouragement to grasp and hold fast the hope appointed for us and set before [us].

> [Now] we have this [hope] as a sure and steadfast anchor
> of the soul [it cannot slip and it cannot break down under
> whoever steps out upon it—a hope] that reaches farther and
> enters into [the very certainty of the Presence] within the veil.
>
> HEBREWS 6:18–19, AMP

Having run to God for refuge, we fasten ourselves to the hope God imparts. We do not look deep into ourselves to find help. We do not fasten ourselves to other saviors. Hope is not wishful thinking. Scriptural hope means expectation; I expect God to come through in some way.

We cry out into the darkness that surrounds us, and He comes! He Himself comes and overtakes us with His heart and His vision. Now we can move with confidence into the future. He is our hope, and Hope has come.

This kind of hope will not slip. It cannot break down, regardless of what happens. It is unsinkable. In Hosea 2:15, the Hebrew word for *hope* means not merely expectation, but a rope or a cord. Hope is the rope that wraps itself around us and pulls us into our future. Like a magnet, it draws us beyond the veil into God's presence. Sure and steadfast, it secures us there.

> When God made his promise to Abraham, he backed it
> to the hilt, putting his own reputation on the line. He said,
> "I promise that I'll bless you with everything I have—bless
> and bless and bless!" Abraham stuck it out and got everything
> that had been promised to him. When people make promises,
> they guarantee them by appeal to some authority above them
> so that if there is any question that they'll make good on the
> promise, the authority will back them up. When God wanted
> to guarantee his promises, he gave his word, a rock-solid guar-
> antee—God *can't* break his word. And because his word cannot
> change, the promise is likewise unchangeable.
>
> We who have run for our very lives to God have every
> reason to grab the promised hope with both hands and never
> let go. It's an unbreakable spiritual lifeline, reaching past all

appearances right to the very presence of God where Jesus, running on ahead of us, has taken up his permanent post as high priest for us.

HEBREWS 6:13–20, THE MESSAGE

More shakings will occur, but when true hope replaces the uncertainties and gnawing fears that arise from traumas, we are then willing to face more difficulty for the sake of the King and His Kingdom.

Just look at the assembly of faith-filled people listed in the "faith champion" chapter of Hebrews 11. Without having seen the fulfillment of their promises, they willingly faced perils that you and I may never face. These champions of the faith were able to move beyond the threat of the present into the hope of the future. Because they had been captured by hope and faith instead of by uncertainty and fear, they were able to face even death without flinching.

Hope's Incubator Is Uncertainty

Consider Abraham, who because of his faith in God, kept moving forward into the unknown future. He never saw his seed multiply as the sands of the sea. Abraham lived and died having procured only the first part of his prophetic promise. Yet from our vantage point in history, we see how he did in fact inherit his promise by faith. In the face of mountainous uncertainty, he knew God's Word was true.

The incubator of Abraham's hope was his uncertainty. Human reasoning was insufficient. Human effort resulted in major mistakes (and Abraham did try to make the promise happen on his own). His ongoing uncertainty created a desperation for answers. It was more than an intimacy with God issue—it was an answer issue.

The times in which you and I live are no more uncertain than Abraham's time or the time of Jesus' disciples. What can we learn from those who have gone before us? They trusted in the unchanging God and were willing to help establish His Kingdom on earth, in spite of—or maybe because of—the uncertainty and violent upheavals all around. "From the days of John the Baptist until now the kingdom of heaven suffers violence, and the violent take it by force" (Matthew 11:12).

With faith, let's cry out to God for ourselves, as well as for our society. God holds the keys to the future. As it was with the Israelites, this time of upheaval is personal and corporate at the same time. (After all, *corporate* means "body," and a body is, by definition, composed of individual parts.)

A genuine heart cry arising from our desperation will reach heaven. Answers will begin to break through the fog of uncertainty. The Kingdom that you and I are part of is unfolding. It is emerging now. The King to whom we cry is greater than every natural disaster, personal trauma or malicious intent. He is the Immovable Certainty. He is releasing Kingdom understanding and revelation to those who desperately cry out to Him. He is replacing desperate uncertainty with faith in His overarching purpose—the coming of His Kingdom to overtake every other kingdom.

Find Your Door

NOT LONG AGO, the head of an apostolic network in Asia invited me to visit Japan to speak to a group of leaders. I had already started feeling that God wanted me to return to Japan soon, so when I got the invitation, I said yes.

There was only one problem. "We need you, Barbara Yoder, to break us into a new place," the man who issued the invitation explained. "God gave us a prophetic word that you are the one to come and break us through."

I felt about as close to breaking through to a new place as the man in the moon. My own breakthrough was eluding me—how could I help others?

So as I flew high over the Pacific on the way to Japan, I wondered, *How in the world am I going to accomplish anything?* Yet somehow I sensed that their breakthrough would become mine. I knew that

God is efficient and that sometimes He gives us an assignment that enlarges or transforms everyone involved simultaneously. The Asian leaders needed wisdom, understanding and, most of all, revelation. So did I. They needed a supernatural encounter with God so that they could move forward. So did I. They needed a plan; I did, too. Whatever they needed, I needed.

I reminded myself of what Jesus said: "Give, and it will be given to you. A good measure, pressed down, shaken together and running over, will be poured into your lap. For with the measure you use, it will be measured to you" (Luke 6:38, NIV). *So if I give them what they need, God will give back to me what I need? That sounds like a deal!* I thought.

All of us were on the verge of a breakthrough to something new. That meant that we were approaching an entry place, a gate, a door that would be our entry into the next phase of ministry. Even the entrance represented big changes. Going through it would require new approaches, new ways of reaching people, new designs for ministry for the twenty-first century in North America and in Asia.

Dynamics of Spiritual Breakthrough

Spiritual breakthrough has identifiable patterns and processes of change. We can actually talk about the "dynamics" of spiritual breakthrough.

I love doing word studies because they provide me with different takes on a word so that I can grasp concepts better. The word *dynamic* is derived from the Greek word *dunamis,* which means "breakthrough power." We see *dunamis* used in Acts 1:8: "You shall receive power [*dunamis*] when the Holy Spirit has come upon you." *Dunamis* is also the root word for "dynamite."

The word *dynamic* can be defined as "an underlying cause of change or growth." In engineering, the word relates to movement and implies a force that creates movement affecting equilibrium. Therefore I could say, "Breakthrough changes your equilibrium." In other words, when the change of a spiritual breakthrough comes, initially it disturbs your equilibrium. When the change has taken effect fully, you achieve a new equilibrium.

A dynamic is a pattern or process of change, growth or activity, as in "population dynamics." In music, one might speak about a piece as being dynamic, which means that there is variation and contrast in intensity, ebb and flow. Is that not also what we experience in a time of change? The dynamics of change fluctuate from strongly intense to barely discernible.

If I say I have a dynamic life, I mean that my life is filled with energy, power and ability. When something is dynamic, it is usually marked by continuous and productive activity. For example, New York City is a dynamic city. When Motown was in Detroit, it was part of what made Detroit a dynamic city. When you meet someone with a dynamic personality, you find that person forceful in a positive sense—he or she is influential and energetic. To be dynamic is to be alive, functioning, living, operative, running, working, activating, energizing and vitalizing. I love all of those words.

The opposite of dynamic is *static*, which means "remaining the same, maintaining the status quo." So something that is dynamic is *not* maintaining the status quo, but rather is alive, doing what it is intended to do, moving things forward, creating change.

The Dream

As I was preparing to leave on that trip to Japan, my assistant had a dream. God regularly speaks to her in dreams, and in this one she saw the *Titanic* sinking. It was a dramatic scene. She viewed it as if she were watching a video or movie. She saw people scrambling for the lifeboats. Some did not make it; others were holding on for dear life. She told me that in her dream, she and the Lord communicated:

> I asked the Lord, "What is that?"
> The Lord said to me, "That is the Church. The people are still holding on to the dream ship that sank. Many of My people are holding on to the ship they thought was the dream, many are still holding on to the memory of the ship, the dream of what the ship would accomplish, many are still stuck in the memory of a sinking ship. But I have sunk that ship. I had to sink your ship so that you could sail with me."

My assistant went on to tell me,

> I believe the interpretation is pretty clear. Think of all that was invested in the *Titanic*. It was the "dream ship." Many believed it would usher them into the future. Think of everything it represented—it was a vision, it was a dream that ended in a very traumatic event and was completely destroyed. Think of the effects it had on the people who invested into that dream—some committed suicide because they could not handle the dream being destroyed. It was symbolic of many things: wealth, vision, pride and more.

The *Titanic* was luxurious, magnificent, remarkable. It represented the future of ocean travel. Many people wanted to board the *Titanic* for its maiden voyage. Those who could book passage were thrilled. However, in spite of the *Titanic* being an incredible creation of human ingenuity and effort—touted as unsinkable—it sank. As I pondered my assistant's dream, I realized that God was saying, "I have sunk the Church/ministry luxury liner of the past twenty years or more."

What once carried our lives and our future is now finished. It has sunk or is sinking. Because it was so glorious, so phenomenal, and because such amazing things happened there, people flocked to join it, and it has been hard to let go. I did not want to let go. I did not think that I should let go. Yet to get into the new "ship," I needed to let go of the one that had sunk. I needed to get on God's dream cruise.

"Church" as we have known it has lost its glory, its power, its influence. God is unveiling a whole new kind of Church comprised of people who understand that they do not "go to church"; they *are* the Church. Some of them are even worshiping in homes now. Whatever form it takes, the purpose of the Church is to release the Kingdom of God. When Jesus described His ministry, He said it was to teach, preach and release the Kingdom of God. Today, He is restoring the Church to its intended power and influence.

Composed of a multitude of individuals, the Church is therefore both corporate and individual. For its corporate influence to be transformed, *individuals* must change. That means you and I must change.

When God got ready to deliver Israel out of Egypt, the pressure to change was both on Israel as a national entity as well as on each individual. Although the ultimate purpose was to transform Israel into a Kingdom-advancing nation that would conquer other kingdoms, each Israelite had to view it in a very individual and personal way.

Corporately and individually, the people of Israel had to change— dynamically—from living their predictable lives in Egypt to undertaking a wilderness trek in which every day carried a new death threat. Normal life would become seemingly impossible. The Israelites would become miserable. Clearly, this represented a change in their lives. They were standing at the door to their future.

Find the Door

One afternoon I was studying the Word, preparing to preach the following Sunday. All of a sudden, a phrase jumped out at me:

"Now the Lord appeared to Abraham by the oaks or terebinths of Mamre; *as he sat at the door of his tent* in the heat of the day" (Genesis 18:1, AMP, emphasis added).

Abraham sat in his doorway, and that is where God appeared to him. The door of his tent became the entry place for the new move of God. Sitting at his door, Abraham positioned himself for change.

Just before this, God had told Abraham that Ishmael, the son he had conceived with his wife's maid, Hagar, was *not* the promised son (see Genesis 17). God had reiterated His covenant with Abram, changing his name to Abraham and his wife's name from Sarai to Sarah. Those name changes were prophetic concerning God's destiny for their lives. God had also made it clear that since His purposes could not be fulfilled by Ishmael, they would end up being fulfilled through a son yet to be born, one whom Abraham and Sarah would conceive together—and that this would happen in spite of their advanced age. This unborn son represented the next stage of the future. His birth would catapult Abraham (and humankind) a giant leap forward toward ultimate destiny.

This news blew Abraham away. He was elderly, almost one hundred years old, and his wife was ninety. How in the world could they conceive a child? How on earth could Sarah bear a son? What was he supposed to do to make it happen? Was there some herbal medicine growing next to their tent, a bush whose leaves or bark could renew their youth? This was beyond impossible. Yet God had said it. . . .

Abraham was stunned. In the middle of one stifling hot day, he went and sat in his doorway. That was all he could think of to do. That doorway was not where he and his wife would conceive the child, but it was the opening to their tent, the place of conception. That door was the entrance to conception.

This is the very thing you and I must do—simply go to the door that is open to us and sit there. That is what I did when I went to Japan. I put myself on an airplane and sat in the next "doorway." Doing that not only opened up revelation to me, but it also helped position me for my next thrust of ministry.

Paul said, "I press toward the goal for the prize of the upward call of God in Christ Jesus" (Philippians 3:14). In other words, Paul kept taking the next step, the step after that and then the following step. He did not give up, stop or back up. He pressed through every door, pressing toward the goal.

When I started out in ministry, I was basically alone. Then I started meeting people and connecting with them. I just kept going through the doors that opened to me. Some were open for only a short period of time; they were short-term connections. But each door led to a new door, including those that were open for only a short time. And each door I entered led to a bigger "room." Each new room contained more people, more anointing, more influence. Each door led closer to the ultimate goal of fulfilling the purpose for my life. And I am still going through new doors.

God-Encounters Happen at the Door

Doors are powerful. When Abraham positioned himself at the entrance of his tent, not going inside yet, God approached him at the door. This time, He came in a vision. ("Now the Lord *appeared* to Abraham . . .")

The same thing happens with us. At the door, God comes to us in a new way. He reassures and strengthens us, repeats His plan, reveals more details, prods us, provides understanding and connects us with the right people. But most importantly, He just plain *comes* to us. In the doorway, we encounter Him.

When I arrived at the door of Japan, I encountered Him. In Japan, my door was a tiny, very clean, utilitarian hotel room, and the presence of God overwhelmed me there. Engulfed in His presence, waves of revelation began to sweep over me. I began to see connections I had never seen before, understand things I had never understood, rethink paradigms and more. God showed up at my door.

He will do the same for you as an individual, and also for groups of people whom He wants to retool for new achievements. God met the group of 120 believers in the Upper Room at Pentecost. The Upper Room was their door, the door to their city and the door, eventually, to the world. God met Moses at a burning bush; that was the first door of the Exodus.

Warfare at the Door

When Abraham sat in the door of his tent, he could not just take it easy. We will find, as he did, that at the threshold of something new a tug-of-war erupts within us, a vacillation, a back-and-forth pulling. This produces more than a momentary hesitation. Opposing forces, even demonic ones, will meet us there.

The Hebrew language uses two words for "threshold." The first is *caph*, which comes from *caphaph*, a primitive root word that means "to snatch away, to terminate."[1] The second word used for "threshold" is *miphtan*, which comes from *pethen*, a root word meaning "to twist as a snake."[2] That word is pronounced like "python" and is where the name of the snake came from.

As you know, pythons kill their prey by twisting their bodies around them to suffocate them. Right at the threshold of your door, the enemy will try to squeeze the life and breath out of you. In other words, Satan will try to choke off revelation. (Prophetic revelation is life-giving, and breath is related to the life of our spirit.) When this happens, you will feel as if you are "dying."

Furthermore, another power—an enemy from within—also will try to terminate your forward progress there. At the door, you must contend with your fears and doubts before you can proceed. Here is how I described it in my book *The Breaker Anointing*:

We lack vision and do not know how to go forward. We feel surrounded by a sense of spiritual darkness or blindness. We have lost our way and it seems as if we are about to die, as if our lights have been punched out. Hope is lost and despair settles upon us like a wet blanket, suffocating and sickening. Forward progress is temporarily halted.[3]

At the door (threshold), you must face this enemy before you can proceed into the new place.

Miracles at the Door

It is worth contending with your fears at the door to a new thing, because God will help you overcome them. Miracles happen there. It may look as though it is too late for the vision to come to pass; you may feel you are too old and all worn out. You may think you lost the opportunity you thought you had or messed up what you did have—but miracles will happen, if you wait for them. God never changes His mind.

Once God had spoken, the only thing Abraham knew to do was to sit in his door and faithfully review God's promises. He knew God would have to release the miracle. There was no other way the plan of God could come to pass. Then, through the miraculous power of God, the age factor was overridden, and Sarah conceived Isaac. We, too, must review God's prophetic promises and remember that miracles do happen at the door.

The Unfolding Process

As Abraham sat in the door to his tent, he was aligning himself with God's purposes. Tents are tabernacles, places where God's presence comes in an overwhelming way. Abraham positioned himself at the door to the place where God would overwhelm him with His power, grace and supernatural ability.

What does this mean in your life? How can you align yourself?

What is your door? Your door may not be a literal door, but rather a symbolic one. You position yourself for the next thing. If you know you are supposed to move to a certain place, you may begin to make plans, pack your possessions, contact people and look for a new place to live. Your actions align you with God's plan, and they represent your door.

Abraham was *sitting* as he aligned himself with God's purposes. By sitting, he was resting in God's provision. When we sit in our own doors, we rest in Christ Jesus:

> But God, who is rich in mercy, because of His great love with which He loved us, even when we were dead in trespasses, made us alive together with Christ (by grace you have been saved), and raised us up together, and made us *sit together in the heavenly places in Christ Jesus.*
> *EPHESIANS 2:4–6, EMPHASIS ADDED*

When we sit in our doorways, we can view life from heaven's perspective. We are confident, expectant and filled with faith. When we sit, we cease from striving. In order to sit, we must rest on something. Abraham was resting on God's promises, and so do we. Abraham did not have to run around anxious and fearful, trying to make something happen. Neither do we.

Abraham had no seed left, nothing with which to conceive. His sitting indicated that he was trusting God. Far from being lazy or "sitting down on the job," Abraham knew that it was simply time to sit still at the door and let God do the impossible.

In the original version of Genesis 18:1, the word for "door" is *pethach.* That word means entrance, opening, entryway or place. The root word is *pathach,* which means to open wide (literally or figuratively), by loosening, plowing or carving.[4]

Do you see how this helps us understand what can happen at the door? At the door, old structures, patterns and mindsets will be loosened from you. You will change. You will plow your way into God's plan as you become free from attachments to people and former positions, sins, fears, a "quitter" mentality, old ideas about how life should be or what your future should look like, and more.

As you sit in your door, you carve out a new picture of what your future will hold. A new "seer" ability or anointing will come over you. You will see everything with fresh eyes. You may find yourself on a new journey into a whole new line of work. Abraham saw a different future when he parted company with Lot. I know a worship leader who became an entrepreneur and a writer who became an artist. They found themselves on different paths, beginning new careers. God began to bless them in unimaginable ways.

Expect things to open wide at the door. Expect to become aware of abilities or aspects of your personality that have been bottled up inside. You may find business ideas, innovations, new songs, revelation, new attitudes, identity clarification, connections, confidence and much more beginning to break forth—right at the door. You will enjoy new freedom as you let go of old things that you have been holding on to. You will feel different, free. All the painful stresses of the recent past will subside in your memory. You are like a corked champagne bottle from which the cork has suddenly flown out of the opening. The internal pressure had become more than that bottle could bear, and now nothing stops the bubbles (ideas, plans) that are bubbling up and out.

You will have put off old things in order to put on new ones. Biblically, clothes represent identity and attitudes. Yours will be changing. Purposefully, you can put on the garment of praise. Now you can step into a new identity and move forward with fresh confidence. You may discover hidden treasures and inclinations that you did not know you had.

Over the years, I have received several prophetic words about breaking into a revival-type miraculous anointing. I have not been able to figure out what that means. Yet as I have ministered in certain places, I have sensed God nudging me to set my message aside and let Him direct me. When that has happened, I have tapped into a ministry style that is very different for me. The audience responds, things begin to happen—in fact, miracles break out. I seem to step into some realm or new place in which God can use me in fresh ways. He draws something out of me that I had not experienced before and did not know was there.

Sitting at the door, a type of plowing occurs. While you sit there struggling and waiting, your soul will be enlarged. The very character of Christ will be carved into you. New trenches for God's presence and power will be dug out. This is not comfortable. You plow up the hard, unbelieving ground in your life using the Word, prayer, worship, praise and prophetic words. Declaring what God has said to you about the future, you break through to a tangible awareness of the presence of God, and you discover a fresh anointing.

The Anointing Breaks the Yoke

Isaiah wrote,

> It shall come to pass in that day
>> That his burden will be taken away from your shoulder,
>> And his yoke from your neck,
>> And the yoke will be destroyed because of the anointing oil.
>
> ISAIAH 10:27

The *New American Standard Bible* translates it this way: "the yoke will be broken because of fatness [anointing]." The anointing is both the Holy Spirit abiding within you, as well as that tangible sense or awareness of God's presence with you. As you prepare for a new place, you will encounter God's presence more frequently and in greater degree. He will overtake you at times. This is how He helps you move forward.

As God overtakes you, the burdens of uncertainty, confusion, wandering, wondering, outdated and no-longer-anointed positions in which you have served all break off of you. In their place, you find God's presence. This is part of becoming "fat" with God, filled up with Him. That fatness breaks the yoke that has been around your neck. The head is the command center of the body, and whatever controls the neck, controls the head. The hand of the enemy will be dislodged from your neck.

None of this can happen if you are clutching your past status and your accomplishments. You may feel more secure if you hang on to those old things, but in the end your spirit will die.

Some people find such changes so drastic that they are frightened, even tormented. For them, even getting into a sitting position at the door requires a battle. In the book of Judges, Deborah said that there was war at the door (gate) because the people had turned to other gods (see Judges 5:8). What are our "other gods"? They are whatever controls us and keeps us from pressing through and breaking into our next place. They can come from our own flesh or from a demonic presence.

Desperation Wins

At the door, you may want to quit. You may want to turn back. The lack of clarity, the oppression and depression, the conflicts within and without, the self-doubts, the hope deferred, the sense of loss—it is almost too much for you. The struggle saps your motivation. Eventually, it makes you desperate.

Desperation is a great motivator. Desperation makes you cry out to God. It makes you go to war for your future. Abraham found his door and sat down in it, perplexed and mystified. Then, his eyes

wide with wonder, he saw God right there in front of him. The plan
was revealed. His encounter with God propelled him toward God's
plan and purpose for him and for the world that God had placed
him in. His questions were laid aside. Now Abraham could move
forward.

Paul talked about the same thing in a different way. Like him,
we need to move forward and be able to say,

> The things I once thought were so important are gone
> from my life. Compared to the high privilege of knowing
> Christ Jesus as my Master, firsthand, everything I once thought
> I had going for me is insignificant—dog dung. I've dumped it
> all in the trash so that I could embrace Christ and be embraced
> by him. I didn't want some petty, inferior brand of righ-
> teousness that comes from keeping a list of rules when I could
> get the robust kind that comes from trusting Christ—God's
> righteousness.
>
> I gave up all that inferior stuff so I could know Christ per-
> sonally, experience his resurrection power, be a partner in his
> suffering, and go all the way with him. . . . I'm not saying that I
> have this all together, that I have it made. But I am well on my
> way, reaching out for Christ, who has so wondrously reached
> out for me. Friends, don't get me wrong: By no means do I
> count myself an expert in all of this, but I've got my eye on the
> goal, where God is beckoning us onward—to Jesus. I'm off and
> running, and I'm not turning back.
>
> So let's keep focused on that goal, those of us who want
> everything God has for us.

PHILIPPIANS 3:7–15, THE MESSAGE

The Cry

BETWEEN 300,000 AND 417,000 American soldiers lost their lives in World War II. By the end of the war, nearly every American family was mourning the death of a loved one or a neighbor. Daily newspapers listed the deaths of local servicemen, and the news on the radio gave battle details and reports of dire developments.

In Detroit, a pall of fear and death settled over the city as its young men went to war, often straight out of high school—many never to return. Families were being shattered and torn apart by grief and despair. The mother of one of my friends felt she had to do something about it.[1]

My friend Patricia Beall Gruits still remembers the day her brother went off to war. He was just eighteen years old, still "wet behind the ears," in many ways more like a boy than a man. The whole family went with him to the neighborhood drugstore, the collection point for departure. There the local young men had gathered to wait for the bus that would take them to their military assignments.

Their families had come with them. Some were clinging to each other, weeping uncontrollably. Others stood in total silence. No words could explain how they felt. The war's death statistics predicted the probable end of each young man's story. The families knew they were sending their sons and brothers off on a death assignment.

Every member of Patricia's family was weeping. She remembers seeing her little brother, Harry, standing there crying buckets of tears. He had heard everyone talking about the war, and he was inconsolable about losing his beloved older brother. Would he ever see his big brother again?

In this dreadful and terrifying time, their mother, Myrtle D. Beall, who in the 1930s had led Bible classes and prayer groups and who had founded a neighborhood Sunday school that had become a small church, decided to accept an offer to minister on the radio, broadcasting live from the church building. She called the program *America to Your Knees*. Beall's single-minded goal was to summon an army of wartime pray-ers every weekday morning from 10:00 to 10:30. She was not about to do it alone; she was going to find everyone she could in the listening area to pray with her.

After her radio broadcast, Myrtle went straight to the church sanctuary to lead a live prayer meeting from 10:30 to noon. She was joined not only by church members, but also by many people who prayed with her on the radio program. They were desperate. They did not want their sons to die. Some of those listening on the radio had already lost their sons and were stricken with grief, but still they came to pray. They would cry out to God, praying until they saw results.

As these pray-ers met together daily, they learned to pray

through their grief to faith. Faith began to arise as they learned to cry out to God and connect with Him from their hearts. They learned how to pray until God spoke to them, and then they learned to proclaim His words back to Him. Their prayer-cries got God's attention because they had learned to speak out the prayers He had planted in their hearts.

A sound was released in those prayer meetings that caused heaven to overtake hell on the earth. Hell's assignments were interrupted on a daily basis as those people prayed earnestly and faithfully. Jesus put it this way: "Your kingdom come. Your will be done on earth as it is in heaven" (Matthew 6:10).

The war ended, and all 84 of the servicemen from the church, Bethesda Missionary Temple, returned home safely. Not one soldier from that church lost his life.

The people of the church had completed that assignment successfully, but they kept on praying. Something much grander began to unfold. They had gone way beyond the place where they did not want to pray. Now they loved to pray; they could hardly wait to pray. Why? As my friend aptly described it, they stopped feeling as though they were talking to a stranger when they prayed. They personally experienced God, who cared and intervened.

Then in 1948, the unimaginable happened. One Sunday morning, God poured out His Spirit upon them in a way that was totally new. Suddenly, the entire congregation was ushered into a brand-new place, a place they had never been before. When they began to worship, an unusual sound, an angelic choir, joined with them. Revival broke out. For five years they experienced an unprecedented revival. Bethesda became a significant locale in what was known as the Latter Rain Revival. During that time, church attendance increased from a few hundred to a few thousand. The Kingdom came in power.

Revive Us Again

We are at a similar juncture today. Especially after a crisis hits, people seem immobilized with fear of impending doom, with a sense of hopelessness. In this present time of crisis, financial savings have evaporated, homes have been foreclosed and formerly flourishing businesses have been shut down. Entire retirement accounts have disappeared overnight. People see their future going up in smoke. It is easy for fear to grip their hearts. Death is coming in through the windows.

I have told you that in my book *The Overcomer's Anointing*, I wrote at length about how when God gets ready to bring us into a new era, the lights must go out on the old. A type of death must occur both personally and corporately. When the lights go out, it is not at all pleasant. The darkness is palpable.

World War II marked the end of one era and the beginning of another. Human pain and critical need drove both individuals and the Church to a new place of prayer. Out of that season of excruciating difficulty, people desperate for answers cried out to God. What was the result? Revival broke out in 1948 when both the Latter Rain Revival and the Healing Revival were released. Furthermore, as the times began to change, the nation evolved into one where education and a higher standard of living flourished. People experienced a new level of prosperity and comfort. It was not only a material prosperity, but a way of life, a place of fulfillment and enjoyment.

We are now at the end of that era of unusual prosperity. We have come to another juncture. Something has dried up; it is time to cry out again. God warns people not to forget where wealth and prosperity come from—from Him alone (see Deuteronomy 8). Nevertheless, people always forget. Lulled into complacency by the very blessings He sends, taking everything for granted, even Christians have assumed that simply living a basic good life would lead to endless security and prosperity. I have made this assumption. I believed that if I would honor God, work hard and become everything I could be, everything would be all right. I did not grasp that God was after something far deeper, nor did I understand what it meant for His Kingdom to come.

Historically, times of overwhelming darkness, trouble and evil overtake us at critical junctures. This is not just a modern-day phenomenon. To the people experiencing it, things always seem worse than before. In past seasons of great difficulty, what did people do to turn the tide from darkness to a spiritual awakening? They prayed, but what did that look like?

One common denominator throughout history seems to be that *desperation motivates people to cry out to God.* All the revivals or awakenings I have read about occurred in desperate times. In this country, the first Great Awakening in the 1700s occurred at a very low time in American history. The colonies were in a mess. The youth had become rebellious, and morals were at an all-time low. George Whitefield and many others were at the center of that move of God. Then in the wake of the American Revolution, conditions deteriorated again. This drove leaders from many denominations to come together on a regular basis to pray for revival. By 1800, the second Great Awakening had started to turn the nation upside-down. This protracted revival launched camp meetings, the modern missionary movement, the abolition of slavery, the Sunday school movement, Bible societies and more.

Yet again, revival fires burned low. By the mid-1800s, economic disaster brought businesses to their knees. One man started the Fulton Street Revival in New York City by gathering a handful of businessmen every day at noon to pray for the city and the nation. Before the end of the first winter, his one dedicated prayer group had mushroomed into a movement, filling every church and meeting room in the city of New York and springing to life throughout New England.[2]

On the Brink of Disaster, Look Up

This is just a very small sampling of what can happen when prolonged crises create in people a desperation for change. Desperation motivates people to cry out to God. When that crying out evolves into a genuine heart cry that God hears, as He heard the children of Israel cry out in Moses' time, things begin to change. God moves into action. He awakens the hearts of people, young and old, all across a city, state or nation. I believe that this is exactly what is happening today not only in the United States, but globally.

God is preparing you and me for a massive move of His Spirit on the order of a global awakening. First come trials and tests beyond measure. Then comes a time of nothing—just an eerie silence. Although people have been motivated and mobilized to pray and cry out to God and although they have faith, they find themselves in a void or near-vacuum in the spiritual realm. They feel they have lost their mooring point. They cannot hear God's voice, and they cannot communicate well with each other, feeling instead alone in a crowd.

I have become convinced that God is never nearer than at times like this. Out of His mercy, He arranges the perfect environment of spiritual and emotional destitution. Why? *So that His people will cry out to Him.*

God is listening for a unique sound, a sound that says, "This is killing me, but I am going to see this process completed. I *will* bring this thing to birth." The singular sound that heaven is waiting to hear is the cry of pain rolled together with faith.

This is similar to what happens in childbirth. When a woman is ready to bring forth her new child, she enters into a very alone time. Solo, she enters the phase of the birthing process where everything depends on her effort. She can become desperate, even noisy and easily agitated. She may cry out or even scream with agony and exertion. Both in childbirth and in prayer, we call it *travail.*

The Kingdom of heaven is released through such travail, which is "violent" or pressing prayer. I described this kind of prayer in the chapter titled "The Violent Spirit" in my book *Taking on Goliath* (Charisma House, 2009). Patricia Beall Gruits says that as a child, when she would see her mother's friends coming to the door, she would run. Otherwise, she knew she might end up in a prayer meeting. She knew that those meetings could get loud and long. She knew that those people would not be praying just nice, sweet prayers in English, but that they would agonize and pray in tongues, sometimes with explosive cries. Heaven would move in, and hell would move out.

People cannot learn how to pray this way in isolation. Their sense of urgency compels them to find others with whom to pray. By uniting their voices in prayer, not only do the participants see that God hears and responds, but they also mentor each other in how to storm heaven with prayer.

In times such as the one we are living in today, learning to pray at this level assumes a new urgency. Together, we can stop the encroaching darkness. God hears our united cries beseeching Him to come and heal, restore and revive. He enables us to teach and encourage each other. We can urge each other, "Do not get off your knees until you hear a word from God for yourself about this!" Together, we declare back to God the words He speaks to our hearts. We do not have to wait for someone to tell us the word; we grab hold of it for ourselves.

When you hear His words for yourself, nothing can steal them from you. Your faith and your determination will increase to such an extent that you will cry out to God for as long as it takes.

Travailing Prayer

This birthing prayer or travailing prayer is the kind of praying that breaks through barriers to release or give birth to something new. This kind of prayer jumps the ruts, the well-worn, furrowed paths of the past season that mire us in quicksand and stop us from advancing. Those furrows are meant to become a launching pad for the next season. But to find the new groove, you have to first break out of the old ruts.

The Bible shows us the progressive growth of strength, faith and glory:

> Blessed is the man whose strength is in You,
> Whose heart is set on pilgrimage.
> As they pass through the Valley of Baca, . . .
> They go *from strength to strength.* .
>
> *PSALM 84:5–7, EMPHASIS ADDED*

> For I am not ashamed of the gospel of Christ, for it is the power of God to salvation for everyone who believes, for the Jew first and also for the Greek. For in it the righteousness of God is revealed *from faith to faith*; as it is written, "The just shall live by faith."
>
> *ROMANS 1:16–17, EMPHASIS ADDED*

> Now the Lord is the Spirit; and where the Spirit of the Lord is, there is liberty. But we all, with unveiled face, beholding as in a mirror the glory of the Lord, are being transformed into the same image *from glory to glory,* just as by the Spirit of the Lord.
>
> *2 CORINTHIANS 3:17–18, EMPHASIS ADDED*

To call forth this progressive increase of strength, faith and glory, we need to participate in the laboring. Hebrews 11:6 tells us, "Without faith it is impossible to please Him, for he who comes to God must believe that He is, and that He is a rewarder of those who diligently seek Him." Our approach to God must be impregnated with faith. In other words, we must be able to go beyond the feeling that we are talking to a stranger to knowing that God is real and that He cares. Once we get out of our old ruts of doubt, we can forge new paths of faith and strength.

When I pray, initially I want God's attention more than I want His action. Faith gets God's attention. Then He will intervene, taking action. Another translation of that same verse in Hebrews reads, "You can never please God without faith, without depending on him. Anyone who wants to come to God must believe that there is a God and that he rewards those who sincerely look for him" (TLB).

What Should I Do?

I had a personal experience that delivered me to a new level of both faith and strength. I had accepted an international assignment that seemed beyond my physical ability. Yet I was convinced that God wanted me to go. Because I had had vocal cord surgery several years before, my doctor had given me specific instructions about preaching. I absolutely was not to preach from the platform more than twice a day, and if I had to speak more than twice in 24 hours, I was to avoid doing so over an extended period of days. I limited myself according to his directions to protect my voice because I did not want to risk damaging my vocal cords again. (Still vivid in my memory was my past experience with the vocal cord surgery when my throat swelled so much that I could not swallow. For at least 24 hours, I was terrorized by the feeling of suffocation.)

The zinger was that this international assignment involved disobeying my doctor's orders—big-time! I had faith to speak twice a day for eight days, with the two days off for traveling from city to city by airplane. However, I had been scheduled to speak *three* times a day except on the days I would be flying, when they had me speaking twice. I was to preach a total of nineteen times in eight days. All I could think of was my vocal cords. Just thinking about the proposed speaking schedule, I broke out in a cold sweat. I was not worried about not having enough material to preach; there was no shortage there. It was the physical health issues I had on my mind.

I had to get by myself and find God in this situation. Without Him, I had no faith at all. In fact, I was engulfed in fear. I went to my room and met with Him, laying out the situation before Him and wrestling with it all night long. Without His help, there was no way my voice could endure that amount of strain. Neither did I want to let the conference leaders down. They were great people whom I highly respected.

One after another, questions tumbled into my mind. Was God trying to push me beyond my comfort zone, or was this a trap to cripple my voice for the rest of my life? If I said no, would I ruin the relationships I valued? Was I being stupid if I said yes, or faithless if I said no? I rehearsed over and over the panicky feeling of drowning that I had had after my previous surgery, which made me break out in cold sweats again. I also rehearsed the promises of God.

That agonizing night of indecision and prayer was a type of travail. Finally I broke through. I knew I was supposed to say yes. Even laying hold of the faith to say yes released a new level of strength in me. It was a genuine breakthrough and a clear type of birthing. Furthermore, I learned to use my voice differently through the experience so as to conserve it.

Note that it is never wise to go against doctor's orders unless you are sure that you have heard from God and are skilled in knowing God's voice. I am not advocating that kind of risky action. People have died thinking they were to go against a doctor's orders in the name of faith. However, in my case, after travailing with a cry God heard, I knew exactly what I was supposed to do in regard to my voice and the proposed ministry trip. In this specific instance, it was clear that God wanted me to move ahead.

Commanding God's Attention

Jeremiah was in prison for his faith. He was in a terrible mess. Not only was Israel suffering, but so was Jeremiah, just because he obeyed God. Suddenly, in the middle of the courtyard of the guard, he heard God's voice. Here is what the Lord said:

> This is God's Message, the God who made earth, made it livable and lasting, known everywhere as *God*: "*Call to me and I will answer you.* I'll tell you marvelous and wondrous things that you could never figure out on your own. . . . You're going to look at this place, these empty and desolate towns of Judah and streets of Jerusalem, and say, 'A wasteland. Unlivable. Not even a dog could live here.' But the time is coming when you're going to hear laughter and celebration, marriage festivities, people exclaiming, 'Thank God-of-the-Angel-Armies. He's so good! His love never quits,' as they bring thank offerings into God's Temple. I'll restore everything that was lost in this land. I'll make everything as good as new." I, God, say so.
>
> *JEREMIAH 33:2–3, 10–11, THE MESSAGE, EMPHASIS ADDED*

God spoke to Jeremiah, telling Jeremiah to cry out to Him. Apparently, the only way Jeremiah would see the great and mighty things that were hidden from his sight was if God would reveal them—in response to Jeremiah's request. First, Jeremiah had to call out. If he called out, he would see miracles.

God was telling Jeremiah to approach Him in a way that could command His attention. Jeremiah needed to "call out" in the sense of accosting someone. This is an amazing concept. Evidently, the way to uncover hidden blessings is to determinedly call out or cry out to God.

In the New Testament, Paul writes about the revelation of hidden things:

As it is written:
"No eye has seen,
  no ear has heard,
no mind has conceived
  what God has prepared for those who love him"—but God
has revealed it to us by his Spirit.
  The Spirit searches all things, even the deep things of God.
For who among men knows the thoughts of a man except the
man's spirit within him? In the same way no one knows the
thoughts of God except the Spirit of God. We have not received
the spirit of the world but the Spirit who is from God, that we
may understand what God has freely given us.

1 CORINTHIANS 2:9–12, NIV

Paul indicates that one of the reasons we have the Spirit of God
dwelling inside us is so that we can see the things of the Spirit, the
things that have been freely given to us. Our natural minds do not
see or discern them. The only way we can open up our spirits to
hear God's Spirit is to pray—even cry out—to God.

When the Lord told Jeremiah to call out and He would answer,
Jeremiah did not question whether or not God would follow through.
Of course God would do what He was promising! He might not
answer on a timetable that would suit Jeremiah, but He would
answer. If Jeremiah would call out—and if we will call out, too—
God will answer our cries with action.

I do not like the timetable part! When I travail for answers to
problems, I want immediate breakthroughs—the sooner, the better. Today, if not yesterday. Yet assuredly, true travail guarantees
results.

Going to the Depths

Travailing prayer gives birth to God's creative solutions. This
is the kind of prayer that brings to light new ideas, new believers,
fresh circumstances and transformed lives.

When the word *travail* appears in our English-language Scripture, it has been translated from nine different Hebrew words. This gives richness to its underlying meaning. First and most obviously, *travail* means bringing forth children, delivering babies either as a mother or as a midwife. As such, it indicates pain and labor, even writhing pain. It also can indicate sorrow or woundedness, grief or distress—and prayer for the relief of trouble.

The original Latin word behind the English word *travail* means "torment." The word described a medieval instrument of torture made up of three stakes on which a person could be strung up. No matter how you look at it, travail is an extreme word for a painful situation.

Obviously, travail is uncomfortable. Yet it is a necessary part of life. A woman who is not willing to experience travail will never have children. The prayers of a person who is not willing to travail will not bear results. This does not mean that every prayer is travailing prayer, but it does mean that there are times when we must be *willing* to pray that hard.

Travailing prayer is hard work. It is like labor—sometimes prolonged labor. In a time of travail, you will not feel well. You will not be skipping and dancing, singing or rejoicing. You will be in agony. Sometimes you want to take a break, but you know you cannot, not if you want to stick around to see the results of your labor.

Recognizing Travail

For you and me as believers, travail, though painful, is God's way of inviting us to attain some kind of breakthrough, to birth something totally new, to find a solution to a gnawing problem. God Himself issues the invitation to pray this way.

Often we miss the call from God to travail because we interpret our feelings from a human standpoint. It is easy to mistake travail as an emotional upset, some kind of unwanted burden or heaviness that you want to unload. You may feel agitated, uneasy, frustrated, unsettled or heavy. This vague feeling of dissatisfaction or heaviness may make the invitation to travail seem like oppression or depression.

Yet this kind of heaviness is not from the enemy; it is a burden from the Lord. It is an invitation to co-labor with Christ in the birthing process. It is God's way of notifying you that something needs to change and that you need to "pray this thing through."

Until you comprehend what is going on, you may try to alleviate your feelings with comfort food or whatever you do when you are agitated. You may find yourself pacing, distracted and unable to settle down. If eating does not help, you may go off to the movies to see if you can get some mental relief. Perceiving what your internal discomfort means can take a while.

Though the onset of travail is so uncomfortable that you will try to escape from it, the discomfort will only get worse if you fail to recognize that it is a call from God to pray. How will it get worse? You will become more and more weighed down until you feel crushed under the burden of the feelings. Then you will have a new problem—a barrier will arise between you and God. You may take offense against Him, inwardly complaining, *What in the world are You doing to me? Why are You allowing me to feel this way?*

In other words, we tend to interpret this discomfort as God cutting us off, when the resulting barrier is due to our failure to enter into travail, to obey. So the burden that was intended to lead us into breakthrough prayer simply weighs us down at a greater level.

Another tendency is to enter into self-analysis and introspection, which will lead you down the path of self-condemnation, shame and guilt. In your mind, you can turn your feelings over and over, analyzing everything from *A* to *Z*, trying to figure out what is going on and where you must have gone wrong. And yet all this time, all God was doing was trying to get you to pray.

You might think, *Pray? Pray with all this weight on my heart? Pray when the intensity of my feelings has swallowed up my faith?*

Yes, pray! Travail does not come from your mind or your emotions. It comes from your spirit. God's Spirit is pressing in on you, urging you to cry out in prayer. The only thing that will relieve the relentless discomfort is prayer. So pray, whether or not you know what you are praying about. Your only chance for finding out what it is all about is to pray—although you may never know what your prayers are for, or at least not find out until much later.

I remember one morning when I awoke weighed down with a vague feeling of heaviness. I began to pray, and for a long time I had no idea what I was praying about. After perhaps 45 minutes, I suddenly saw a brief vision of a foreign village. Someone who was sick was being carried on a stretcher into the village. I had no idea where that was or what the situation was. I simply kept praying over that visual image until the burden totally lifted. Maybe a year later, I found myself in the place that I had seen in that prayer. The village leaders had just brought a woman into the village on a stretcher, traveling two and a half days to get her there. She was in labor, and the baby was stuck. We put her into our Land Rover and took her to the nearest hospital, where she successfully delivered her baby. I had prayed that situation through nearly a year before, travailing until the threat of death—the baby's or hers or both—was broken, well in advance of the actual emergency.

Travail's Duration and Results

Travail might last for one hour, one morning, or for days, weeks, even months. One time, when President Bush was serving his first term, I travailed for our nation for months in a row. Naturally, I was not groaning aloud wherever I went. But everywhere, I was pervaded with an uneasy concern that gnawed me inside. I felt troubled, hassled, burdened.

I would pray, and it would not lift. I got others to pray, and still it would not lift. I continued to pray, alone and with others, yet nothing lifted. Finally, after months of praying, I knew I had broken through. I knew that my travail had to do with wisdom for the situation in the Middle East.

When I broke through, the Lord spoke to me that I was to go to Washington, D.C., and do two things. One was to declare over Secretary of State Colin Powell a "shift" regarding the Middle East. How could that ever happen? I was simply a pastor and prayer leader. This was shortly after 9/11. Clearance in the State Department was highly improbable. No one was getting clearance. I contacted a friend in Washington, and she knew what to do. A miracle happened and I got into the State Department.

What next? How in the world now was I going to see Colin Powell? Just as we cleared security and turned the corner, we saw Colin Powell walking down the hall, quite a distance away, coming toward us. As we approached each other, I began to declare under my breath that the shift would take place. As soon as I released that declaration, the burden lifted. To this day, I do not understand it completely. I do not need to. I just know that God put me into a season of travailing prayer so that a breakthrough could occur. And after that, Powell shifted his position.

As in the process of a natural human birth, the process of travailing prayer involves concentrated, cooperative effort. Just as the release of special hormones dilates a mother's birth canal and lubricates the pathway of the baby, so does the labor of travailing prayer open and enable significant changes to occur. In times of concentrated travailing prayer, I have come to recognize the moment when prayer just begins to flow. (I call it the "grease slick.") A special kind of anointing assists in the "delivery" process, and it can be attained only by my cooperation with the travail.

In travailing prayer, the "baby" is some change, some new thing that needs to come forth, something conceived by God. To bring it forth, someone must recognize the "birthing anointing" and enter into travailing prayer. That person must come into agreement with the assignment, whether or not the ultimate results are comprehensible.

You and I cannot decide, "Today, I am going to travail." We must be apprehended by God first. The book of Lamentations contains an interesting statement:

> He drew his bow
> and made me the target for his arrows.
> He pierced my heart
> with arrows from his quiver.
> *LAMENTATIONS 3:12–13, NIV*

Travail is like that. God deliberately shoots an arrow that enters your heart; it captures both your will and your affections. The arrow seems to have a rope on the end of it, which God pulls first one way, then another, to lead you through the process of travail. God, not you or I, decides what that process of birthing will consist of in terms of duration, purpose and details. Travail is a prayer assignment with a specific goal.

Spirit-to-Spirit Response

So what if now I know God has chosen me for one of His birthing projects? What do I do?

First of all, I set aside time to meet with God. I often start with worship. I begin to verbalize my praises, declaring the truth about God's greatness, majesty and love. As I worship, I am presenting myself to God, and I am building my faith in who He is. I am also expressing my inability to solve the problem, yet also saying, "Here I am. I'm available."

Purposely, I begin to build my faith by declaring who He is, reviewing the Word. I begin to rehearse the truths about His miraculous ability to break through any problem, impossible situation or chaotic mess. "You are the God of heaven and earth. You can do anything." In other words, I worship, I bow down before Him and I submit my spirit to His Spirit.

Faith is critical to praying any situation through. I must have unwavering faith that God will see me and this situation all the way through to completion. By exalting God and recounting the facts about who He is, I cause my faith to soar. Sometimes, I literally feel as if I am an airplane taking off.

Next, I begin to talk to God about what is on my mind. I try to put in words what I am experiencing. I describe the concern or the weight that I am feeling, and then I say something like, "Here I am—I am available to pray this thing through!" I start, praying first about the most prominent issue or concern that comes to my mind.

If the presence of God or His anointing does not come to me as I pray over that matter, then I start to pray about the next thing on my mind. I do that until at last I find His presence, and I begin to flow in prayer. Now it is no longer work. I have found the "grease slick." Now I am in travail. The anointing of the Holy Spirit brings me into oneness with Him, and suddenly I am carried along by the power of the Holy Spirit. My praying goes way beyond my understanding:

> God's Spirit is right alongside helping us along. If we don't know how or what to pray, it doesn't matter. He does our praying in and for us, making prayer out of our wordless sighs, our aching groans. He knows us far better than we know ourselves, knows our pregnant condition, and keeps us present before God. That's why we can be so sure that every detail in our lives of love for God is worked into something good.
>
> ROMANS 8:26–28, THE MESSAGE

Always remember that only God can initiate true travail. We can position ourselves for it, but it is God who must take us to that place in prayer. Not only does He instigate travailing prayer for matters of sweeping national importance or for miraculous interventions, He also uses this kind of prayer for the deep work of making disciples. Paul wrote to the people of the church in Galatia:

> My little children, for whom I am again suffering birth pangs until Christ is completely and permanently formed (molded) within you, would that I were with you now and could coax you vocally, for I am fearful and perplexed about you!
> *GALATIANS 4:19–20, AMP*

Bring Forth the New

Every time we enter a new era, travail must occur in some form. Micah wrote, "Now why do you cry aloud? Is there no king among you? Has your counselor perished, that pains have taken you like a woman in labor? Writhe in pain and labor to bring forth . . . like a woman in childbirth" (Micah 4:9–10, AMP). Here travailing and birthing are linked with warfare. The purposes of God in the earth cannot come forth without a war.

When Jesus was in the Garden of Gethsemane, He was in a type of travail. For Him, it was a time of agonized wrestling. He did not want to have to go through anything unnecessary and certainly did not want to suffer needlessly. He wanted to avoid the crucifixion if at all possible. However, if it was the will of His Father, He was willing. Jesus cried out to His Father, offering up "prayers and supplications with strong crying" (Hebrews 5:7, KJV). "Being in agony, He prayed more earnestly. Then His sweat became like great drops of blood falling down to the ground" (Luke 22:44).

Isaiah predicted of our Savior, "He shall see [the fruit] of the travail of His soul and be satisfied . . . for He shall bear their iniquities and their guilt [with the consequences, says the Lord]" (Isaiah 53:11, AMP). By His travail, you and I are free today. Travail is more than prayer; it is the willingness to bear another person's heavy burdens to the point of deliverance.

Nobody gets up in the morning and says, "Today, I want to travail!" It is too uncomfortable, too heavy, too painful. Isaiah expressed it well when he said, "Therefore are my [Isaiah's] loins filled with anguish, pangs have seized me like the pangs of a woman in childbirth; I am bent and pained so that I cannot hear, I am dismayed so that I cannot see" (Isaiah 21:3, AMP). When travail comes, we are totally preoccupied with whatever God has burdened us with. This is no "Sweet Hour of Prayer."

Yet it is worth it. Can you imagine what would happen if we would take travail seriously and follow it all the way through to the finish line? Think about the potential breakthroughs in business, in government, in the Church and in our families! And ultimately, when we have prayed something all the way through, we are so happy that we forget the pain of birthing it. John wrote,

> When a woman gives birth, she has a hard time, there's no getting around it. But when the baby is born, there is joy in the birth. This new life in the world wipes out memory of the pain. The sadness you have right now is similar to that pain, but the coming joy is also similar. When I see you again, you'll be full of joy, and it will be a joy no one can rob from you.
>
> JOHN 16:21–23, THE MESSAGE

We need travailing prayer in this new era in which we find ourselves. Changes must take place. Therefore, an army of travailers needs to go into action, similar to what happened when Myrtle Beall called together her army of intercessors during World War II.

King Jesus, may Your Kingdom come on earth as it is in heaven!

You came once to Bethlehem. May Your Bride be prepared so that You can come again soon. We are longing for the day of Your coming.

> But you, Bethlehem Ephrathah,
>> though you are small among the clans of Judah,
>> out of you will come for me
>> one who will be ruler over Israel,
>> whose origins are from of old,
>> from ancient times.
> Therefore Israel will be abandoned
>> until the time when she who is in labor gives birth
>> and the rest of his brothers return
>> to join the Israelites.
>
>> *MICAH 5:2–3, NIV*

9

The Voice of the Bride

IT WAS GOING TO BE another exciting Saturday. Dad said he was taking the family to the state park to hike, swim and have fun. I could hardly wait. I loved those summer trips. All five of us would pile in the car with our swimsuits and towels, a jug of Kool-Aid with sliced oranges, lemons or limes floating on top, usually a fresh cake baked from scratch (not the box kind, but real cake) and the rest of the fixings for a picnic lunch. Mother had a way of making anything taste good, even plain old Kool-Aid. And her cakes were to die for.

I loved that old Mercury Dad drove, with its leather seats and baby blue interior. Something about it made our family outings seem even more special, and it was sort of homey the way my brother sat in the backseat between my sister and me, while Mother would keep us entertained with classic road-trip games such as counting signs, colors or models of cars, and farm animals. It was the ultimate family time.

I could hardly wait to arrive at the state park. I loved to swim, hike and spend the whole day enjoying fun activities with my family. But first, those familiar words would slip out of my father's mouth: "I have to stop in Columbus on our way and see a customer—but it will just take a moment."

I knew about Dad's moments; they were like hitting this giant pause button. My surging adrenaline would crash to the floor mat. We would take a "little" detour into Columbus, only to sit in the car for a minimum of an hour while Dad did business with a customer. There was no air conditioning in the car. With the windows rolled down, we would sit in the middle of the asphalt parking lot with the heat waves rising around us. That homey backseat did not feel so great anymore. Three hot, sweaty kids would get irritable, thirsty, sometimes hungry and always impatient, putting our pent-up energy into complaining, agitating and elbowing one another. You know how it goes.

Our expectations had been set up for fulfillment—but also for disappointment. Disappointment created family outrage in the family car. We could not wait any longer. Fed up, we would unleash a unified cry from the unbearably hot and sweaty confines of the backseat.

This dreaded scenario happened to me again a little while ago. I was flying back from taping a television series. Feeling great, I was thinking, *I've just pulled off the latest scheduling miracle! My interviews are complete, and I'm on my way back home within 24 hours. . . .*

That train of thought lasted until I hit the Minneapolis airport to change planes. Only one runway was in operation because of construction. The weather was dismal. And the vice president of the United States had decided to fly into that airport the same night. What had started out as an almost-perfect trip suddenly turned into a travesty of delays. Though I had planned to reach home by 9:00 P.M., at 5:00 A.M. the next day I finally dragged my body into my own bed.

Someone had hit the pause button, and I ended up on the waiting list. My beautiful plans had just turned into chopped liver. I played with my iPhone, called whomever I could think of to call, got another something to drink, then collapsed, exasperated, into an airport chair that felt like a lumpy mattress. I was doing the Lord's work, but His part in it did not seem to include taking very good care of me. If I could have gotten the plane off the ground, I would have piloted it myself. Of course, my impatient "let's get this show on the road" attitude only made me even more miserable.

The whole experience gave me another sample of the broader scene we are encountering as we enter this new era. God seems a lot like my earthly father. I did not know that reaching a destination could be so difficult. In fact, like my airline journey, this journey into the new era can sometimes seem convoluted and unnecessarily hampered from a human perspective. It is not simply a case of finding our way into a new place by taking the quick and easy road; this new era has involved some exceptionally long delays and detours for a multitude of reasons.

What should I do? Pretend delays do not matter to me? Wait with my hands folded, a picture of resignation? Whine and complain and throw a tantrum? Or remind myself that my heavenly Father has a plan and a future for me, and that even though I cannot drive the car myself (or the plane, or the universe), I am more than willing to do whatever it takes—including some more fidgety waiting in the backseat—to help Him achieve His goal.

Patiently Impatient

I have been describing our present situation as the beginning of a new era, and I have compared it to being given a blank book to write in. It can seem intimidating, faced as we now are with the stark white, blank pages of a book that you and I have the responsibility of filling with the right story. Yet people just like us have accomplished this daunting task many times over the years in their own "new" eras. We can read their stories in the historical and biblical records, and find encouragement.

Paul called our Father the "God of all comfort," and His comfort and encouragement shine through in the most challenging stories of His past dealings with people. In fact, something about the difficulties contributes to the sense of comfort:

> Blessed be the God and Father of our Lord Jesus Christ, the Father of mercies and God of all comfort, who comforts us in all our tribulation, that we may be able to comfort those who are in any trouble, with the comfort with which we ourselves are comforted by God. For as the sufferings of Christ abound in us, so our consolation also abounds through Christ. Now if we are afflicted, it is for your consolation and salvation, which is effective for enduring the same sufferings which we also suffer. Or if we are comforted, it is for your consolation and salvation. And our hope for you is steadfast, because we know that as you are partakers of the sufferings, so also you will partake of the consolation.
>
> *2 CORINTHIANS 1:3–7*

When I read that passage not long ago, it dawned on me that we are on the same journey that God's people have been on throughout biblical history. Many books have been written about what transpired in earlier times. That recorded history provides clues for us in our present journey.

Historical Perspective for the Journey

In the Garden, God gave Adam and Eve a mandate. This was a personal and corporate mandate to humankind, male and female.

God commanded them to do five things: bear fruit, multiply, fill the earth, subdue the earth and take dominion:

> Then God blessed them, and God said to them, "Be fruit-ful and multiply; fill the earth and subdue it; have dominion over the fish of the sea, over the birds of the air, and over every living thing that moves on the earth."
>
> **GENESIS 1:28**

This mandate is both progressive and aggressive. It involves much more than bearing children and cultivating crops. Because our children inherit our DNA, they inherit the mandate to subdue the earth by taming creation, restraining warring forces, pacifying concerns, subjugating rebels and eventually progressing to the stage of dominion.

The foundational mandate of the Church is to help bring in the dominion of the Kingdom of God. The Kingdom of God overcomes every other kingdom. According to the second chapter of Daniel, a stone has been cut out of the mountain (Jesus) and it is becoming a great mountain (kingdom) that fills the whole earth:

> You watched while a stone was cut out without hands, which struck the image on its feet of iron and clay, and broke them in pieces. Then the iron, the clay, the bronze, the silver, and the gold were crushed together, and became like chaff from the summer threshing floors; the wind carried them away so that no trace of them was found. And the stone that struck the image became a great mountain and filled the whole earth.
>
> **DANIEL 2:34–35**

The Overcomer, Jesus, loves a Bride, the Church, and the final outcome has been stated this way in Revelation 11:15: "The king-doms of this world have become the kingdoms of our Lord and of

His Christ, and He shall reign forever and ever!" Ultimately every kingdom will bow to the one Kingdom, the Kingdom of God, ruled by the King of kings. That is ultimate dominion. Jesus, who was referred to as the stone that the builders rejected, has become the chief cornerstone (see Psalm 118:22–23; Matthew 21:42).

War Over the Mandate

The war over this mandate is one of the underlying themes of all Scripture. This war shows up from Genesis to Revelation. It is a conflict between God Himself and the ruler of this world, Satan. It encompasses religious, governmental and economic systems. It pits the Bride of the Garden against the harlot in the wilderness (see Revelation 17). Ultimately, the Bride's inheritance will be the Garden, and the harlot's will be the wilderness—which represents the ultimate in restoration. In the Word of God, we started out in the Garden, and we will also end up there.

The Bride of Christ has been chosen to release the Kingdom of God throughout the earth, restoring dominion and thereby bringing heaven to earth. The harlot represents the rebellious, antichrist power ruling over a world system through the three-fold cord of religion, political power and the world economic system. She ends up impoverished and empty, living in a desolate wasteland. She will be brought down by Jesus through His Bride, the Church.

So the ultimate war of kingdoms—unfolding in unparalleled dimensions in our day—is the Bride versus the Harlot. The Bride, surrendered to her King, contends with the Harlot, submitted to the king of darkness, Satan or Lucifer, who lost his place in heaven.

On a microcosmic level, that means you and I, as individual members of the Bride of Christ, are involved in something far beyond what we can see, hear or comprehend. We are involved in a cosmic war for control, and it plays out every day across the world on every level, from the privacy of individual bedrooms to the highest levels of international systems. It is an unseen war of kingdoms:

> We speak wisdom among those who are mature, yet not the wisdom of this age, nor of the rulers of this age, who are coming to nothing. But we speak the wisdom of God in a mystery, the hidden wisdom which God ordained before the ages for our glory, which none of the rulers of this age knew; for had they known, they would not have crucified the Lord of glory.
>
> *1 CORINTHIANS 2:6–8*

Jesus Himself said that He would build His Church and that the gates of hell would not prevail over it (see Matthew 16:18). He has left His Church (His Bride) on earth to complete what He started when He released His power and authority to take back the earth. Ultimately the Church will win the battle, and the Kingdom of God will overtake every other kingdom. That is true dominion:

> Then comes the end, when He delivers the kingdom to God the Father, when He puts an end to all rule and all authority and power. For He must reign till He has put all enemies under His feet. The last enemy that will be destroyed is death. For "He has put all things under His feet." But when He says "all things are put under Him," it is evident that He who put all things under Him is excepted. Now when all things are made subject to Him, then the Son Himself will also be subject to Him who put all things under Him, that God may be all in all.
>
> *1 CORINTHIANS 15:24–28*

Why have I reiterated all of this? Because this drama is building in intensity and in critical mass as we move closer to the end of this age. It is time for the real Church to emerge with spiritual revelation and understanding about what is actually transpiring. It is time for the voice of the Bride to be heard as never before.

As believers, it is all too easy to become engulfed and entangled in the natural thinking of this world, to see our lives from a natural rather than a spiritual perspective. No wonder we wander through life, blind as bats about what is really going on. No wonder we fail to enter into our real call, our purpose for being. We live with frustration, small-mindedness and empty faith, constantly seeking something that will fulfill us. We accommodate to the systems and thinking of this age, blinded by them and failing to see the real purpose of God, which is the fulfillment of the Genesis 1:28 mandate. Ultimately, He wants us to become a people who have progressed from one couple (Adam and Eve) to an entire Kingdom that overcomes every other kingdom.

The two kingdoms referred to as the Bride and the Harlot are portrayed as women because they have power to give birth, as well as to fight for the hearts and minds of a generation. The Harlot is entirely self-seeking. She seduces, deceives, prostitutes and plunders all she can. She strips men, women, cities and nations of their dignity and worth. She wants to control them for her own gain, so she holds them prisoner (see Isaiah 14:4–27). The Bride, on the other hand, gives herself away to the One who so loved the world that He gave His life for it. She loves, releases truth, births true disciples and builds up. She restores people, cities and nations. She is the embodiment of freedom on the earth.

God is looking for individuals who will allow Him to break them out of the nations, cultures and systems that they have been accustomed to, so that they can break into and war against kingdoms ruled by the Harlot. You and I are involved in this kingdom war. Our mandate remains progressive, from bearing fruit to ultimate dominion. Our mandate is to unite our minds and hearts to take the land and possess it, developing it as a territory under the rule of the King of kings.

Part of that process involves the shift from a personal, local church with an "us four and no more" mentality to a Kingdom paradigm. Although as an individual I may comprehend the mandate idea, how do I fit into the bigger scheme set forth in Scripture? What do the Bride and the Harlot have to do with me?

To begin with, you and I must shift paradigms. We must stop "going to church" and *become* the Church.

Breaking into a New Paradigm

Scripture is jam-packed with examples, one after another, of God breaking individuals and groups, even whole nations, out of their old paradigms or belief systems that kept them from fulfilling His ultimate mandate. We know all of the stories, but we may never have viewed them in this light. Consider Abraham. He was a heathen the first time he encountered God. That encounter transformed him. Delivered out of an idol-worshipping culture, Abraham built a new life of obedience to and worship of the one true God.

Abraham left his familial land and wandered about looking for Canaan, for a city "whose builder and maker is God" (Hebrews 11:10). He wondered where he would end up. Where was this land that he had been promised? With a barren wife, where was this son who would carry on the inheritance? The journey seemed endless. And then when he got to Canaan, he did not seem to know where he was.

Like us, he wandered until he finally figured out what God was trying to do in and through him. He pushed out into new territory. He knew he had been given a promise, and he pursued it to the best of his ability. And yet Abraham died without ever having possessed the complete promise God had given. Did he understand that he had nevertheless fulfilled God's purposes for his life? Did he realize that he had, in fact, staked a claim on God's promises, and that what he had done in his lifetime had set Kingdom-commanding forces in motion?

Abraham had assented to God's call to travel to an unknown destination that would become his home. He responded in faith to God's words every time God intervened in his life. The whole time, God was creating an entirely new structure and framework for his life and for the lives of those who would follow him. God had delivered him out of an idolatrous system, breaking off ungodly beliefs, values, perceptions and motivations. He had broken Abraham into his purpose in the earth, which was to play a (significant) part to advance a Kingdom that could never be shaken or overcome. The whole time, Abraham operated in faith. Even as he was cooperating with God, he did not really "get it."

Sometimes, like Abraham, I do not get it. I want to knock on the side of my head and ask myself, *Is anyone home?* Other people seem to get it. But I do not. I may know a lot of facts, but what in the world do they mean? I know a lot about the Bible, but until God opens the eyes of my understanding and revelation begins to pour in, I do not understand what I should do with that information.

Abraham's destiny was to bring forth Isaac, and through him to propagate the generations so that the vision could be achieved. He was to become part of the ongoing purpose of God in the earth, to raise up a people who would fulfill the Genesis mandate. God spoke to him and reassured him that, even though he would not live to see the achievement of the goal, his cooperation and persistence would be rewarded:

Then He said to Abram: "Know certainly that your

descendants will be strangers in a land that is not theirs, and
will serve them, and they will afflict them four hundred years.
And also the nation whom they serve I will judge; afterward
they shall come out with great possessions. Now as for you,
you shall go to your fathers in peace; you shall be buried at a
good old age. But in the fourth generation they shall return
here."

GENESIS 15:13–16

Little did Abraham know what God was talking about—that
his descendants (the Israelites) would be trapped in Egypt for four
hundred years after being planted there by his great-grandson
Joseph and seventy family members who had been saved from
starvation. Little did anyone know that those seventy people
would grow into two or three million people who would advance
God's Kingdom plan simply by bearing fruit, multiplying and
filling Egypt with Israelites, becoming a mass of people to be
reckoned with.

Abraham could not have anticipated how things would play out
over time, how in spite of their numbers and destiny, the Israelite
slaves never subdued Egypt, but instead Egypt subdued them, how
Israel prospered so much that Egypt became fearful of them and
began to persecute them. As persecution somehow created prolif-
eration and as Israel prospered more and more, Egypt persecuted
more and more.

> But the harder the Egyptians worked them the more chil-
> dren the Israelites had—children everywhere! The Egyptians
> got so they couldn't stand the Israelites and treated them worse
> than ever, crushing them with slave labor.
>
> *EXODUS 1:12–13, THE MESSAGE*

Abraham could not have known about the turning point that
would finally occur when Pharaoh decided to kill all the male babies

born to the Israelite slaves. This was the straw that broke the camel's
back. Then the Israelites cried out in earnest for deliverance. Until
then, they could always adapt and find a way around their problems.
But sacrificing their babies was too much. At last, a real cry erupted
from them, and it got God's attention:

> Then the children of Israel groaned because of the bond-
> age, and they cried out; and their cry came up to God because
> of the bondage. So God heard their groaning, and God
> remembered His covenant with Abraham, with Isaac, and with
> Jacob. And God looked upon the children of Israel, and God
> acknowledged them.
>
> *Exodus 2:23–25*

God was doing something far more than allowing them to experience intense agitation. He was permitting Egypt to goad them into
a new place. This concerned far more than Egyptian bondage. It had
to do with God's covenant with Abraham and his descendants. It had
to do with the original mandate to Adam and Eve. It pointed the way
toward Israel's destiny to overcome and to take dominion in Canaan.
God's destiny for Israel was not to fight back and subdue Egypt; rather
it was to conquer Canaan. And their destiny was not to coexist in
the Promised Land, Canaan, alongside the Canaanites, but instead
to become the complete possessors of the land. They were to subdue
the occupants of Canaan and bring them under dominion.

That is radical. It is also Scripture. God allowed the Israelites
to become miserable enough that they would be willing to leave
the place where they had become comfortable and prosperous and
move on into their destiny—out of desperation.

Miserably Uncomfortable

To me, *destiny* sounds like a magical, dreamed-about ideal.
If someone offered me the opportunity to possess my destiny,

I would be glad to jump on a plane to go and possess what had been granted to me. But in real life, the process is a little more complicated.

For starters, I tend to value what has become my normal life so much that it masquerades as good and even ideal. I have a job, life insurance, health insurance, good pay, a comfortable home, a nice car, a decent family, a good church and a big-screen TV. I will not easily give that up to take on the conquest of an unspecified future.

The state that I live in, Michigan, used to be the most entrepreneurial state in the nation—one hundred years ago. The people were innovative, risk-friendly and willing to lose all to achieve gain. Now Michigan is the least entrepreneurial and most risk-averse state in the union. Why? Because the lifestyle that innovation brought (I am thinking in particular of the development and production of the automobile) created citizens who did not want to give up their comforts. Consequently, over time, they slid into accommodation with the system, forgot that times and seasons change and accepted what the auto companies produced as an eternal cash cow. Now it is Michigan's turn to cry out. Detroit, at one time one of the four largest cities in the nation, has dwindled from a population of 1.9 million to only 900,000—and it is decreasing daily. The people who had grown comfortable with the fruit of the economic system are now miserable.

God has a plan for Michigan, though, just as He had a plan for Israel. Due to our human nature, we need quite a bit of prodding before we are willing to suffer for the sake of the next step on our journey. The parallel with Israel is not perfect here, but you can grasp my point. For probably all of us, the only thing that will create enough willingness to change is sustained, intense pressure of some sort. Otherwise, we are quite content to stay where we are.

But when the old system that frames our lives becomes unbearable, we just might get up and do something.

Granted, more than one upheaval may be required before we get it. We are quick to call problems "just a test," a temporary setback, a blip on the radar or a misinterpretation. We tell each other, "Just pray, praise, speak the Word and get your attitude right." Or we say, "Take a vacation and get away from all the stress, and soon everything will be hunky-dory again."

Rarely ever do we recognize that God may be shaking us loose from our old, familiar structures and systems in order to make us miserable within the framework we have grown accustomed to. Still less do we recognize that He wants to do away with those all-too-familiar things. We are so unwilling to let go that if we cry out to God at all, we cry out for more grace to live within the misery that has set up camp in our lives.

The real question is not how long the process takes to get to the "new," but whether or not we will cry out to God in utter desperation. When will we stop rallying and accommodating ourselves back to the old system? What will it take to get our attention?

When the structure overtakes the purpose and the vessel through which it flows, then it either has to change or be broken. When a church, for example, exists to maintain itself, you can know that the purpose for which it was founded has become extinct. Now the church exists solely to be taken care of, whereas its original design was to act as the vehicle through which Jesus could flow to people, transforming, strengthening, saving, delivering, equipping and sending them out to change the world.

Immersed in our old, familiar structures, we do not understand what is happening in this new era. No one realizes what God is doing. This cycle of shake-ups and grief keeps accelerating until we cannot find grace any longer. Grace has gone to live in another city. Grace to live with the status quo has gone from our lives for good. Now we do not know whether to blow up the system in which we have been living or blow up ourselves. Blowing up ourselves would be to implode with frustration over circumstances for which we have totally run out of grace, to hit the self-destruct button not in a suicidal sense, but in a figurative sense. Things are reaching a critical point. We have to do *something*.

A fairly long span of time can elapse between the commencement of our discomfort and the expiration date of our grace.

It just may be that we are in such a moment today. A cry is building up.

Kingdom Come

THE NEW TESTAMENT CHURCH was birthed when 120 believers went into the Upper Room to wait for the Holy Spirit to empower them, as Jesus promised (see Acts 1:8). When the promise came, something massive shifted. Like a rushing, mighty wind, the Holy Spirit came into that room and changed the ragtag remnant of Jesus' followers into an army of transformers. They ran down the stairs and into the streets of Jerusalem. That same day, three thousand people were saved. They did not go back upstairs, sign a perpetual lease for the building, construct a steeple on top and make the people come to them there. No, they started the greatest grassroots movement that has ever existed. They went into all the world with the message of the Good News of Jesus Christ.

These days, sometimes our attempts to advance as God's army are not quite so transformational. Today, we find ourselves at a critical juncture in history. God is attempting to change the mind of the Church. Over the years, we have become muddled. We think it is normal to put our lives on autopilot and to suspend inquiries about what God really wants us to do. Our motto is "Don't think or ask questions beyond what you already know." We rarely ask, "What new thing does God want to do right now?" or "How do I fit into that?" or "What is the Church, and how am I supposed to relate to it?" Still less do we wonder how the Church and Kingdom of God interact. We just do not think about it much.

A Massive Retooling

Church as we know it has become a hindrance to fulfilling God's mandate. Instead of liberating people to go out and conquer their promised land, it has become a structure that confines and restricts. It appears to have the order backward. For centuries, Christians have fortified "the Church" as an institution that people must visit, instead of taking the message of the Kingdom out into homes, marketplaces and schools.

We do need gatherings and we need schools to train God's people, but why do we need to capture people inside buildings and create an unspoken and unconscious paradigm of retreating rather than advancing? How are we fulfilling the mandate to subdue the earth and take dominion in the name of the God we worship?

To respond to both God's original mandate and to the urgency of the times we live in, we need to change from a Church paradigm to a Kingdom one. When Jesus walked with His disciples, He did not tell them to start churches, but instead to stay on the move, teaching, preaching and demonstrating the Gospel of the Kingdom. Churches arose as groups of people came together to encourage each other in their new life.

Originally churches, as buildings, were not intended to become retreat centers. They were intended as places where believers could be equipped and empowered, places where they could have covenantal connection with each other and sustain each other. Once believers were equipped, they moved in and out of the church building, and in and out of the marketplace. After being out in the marketplace, people could enter the church building and have their strength and vision renewed. But the building itself was never intended as the be-all and end-all.

In other words, a Kingdom paradigm is not the same as a Church-maintenance mindset. God does not like our assumptions. He is using multiple means to get our attention, and He is shattering our confidence in the structures we have learned to trust.

God has said that He would cover the earth with the knowledge of His glory as the waters cover the sea (see Habakkuk 2:14). This is not just a poetic statement. Already the earth is covered with an ever-growing population of people, and the glory of God inhabits the individuals who name His name. He dwells in a temple not made with hands (see Acts 7:48; 17:24; 1 Corinthians 6:19).

To come along with God on this end-time journey, each one of us needs a new encounter with Him. All of us carry seeds of the future inside us, but they cannot come to fruition without a paradigm-shattering encounter with the living God. Moses encountered God at the burning bush before he picked up his rod and went back to lead the Israelites. David had an encounter when Samuel anointed him with oil and the Holy Spirit came on him. After that, he fought Goliath and entered into the first phase of his public ministry. Joshua had encounters with God before and after Moses died; otherwise he would never have known that God was mantling him to lead the people into Canaan. Gideon had an encounter with the angel of the Lord, or God in an epiphany, when he was challenged to deliver his fellow Israelites. Both Abraham and Sarah encountered God in a new way before the birth of their promised son, Isaac.

These are days of fresh encounters with the living God. Look around you and you will see new revelation, new relationships, new gatherings, new movement and new empowerment, confirmation that a fresh anointing of God's presence and power is streaming down upon us. The people of God are crying out, like David, "I have been anointed with fresh oil" (Psalm 92:10).

Take courage from the patterns you see in Scripture. Often barrenness must be endured before great breakthroughs. Sarah, Rachel, Hannah and others were barren. Their barrenness brought them to a point of critical encounter so that a cry would rise up from them. And from those cries, children would be born who would change the course of history. With that in mind, review the familiar words of Isaiah's prophecy:

"Sing, O barren woman,
    you who never bore a child;
    burst into song, shout for joy,
    you who were never in labor;
    because more are the children of the desolate woman
    than of her who has a husband,"
    says the LORD.
"Enlarge the place of your tent,
    stretch your tent curtains wide,
    do not hold back;
    lengthen your cords,
    strengthen your stakes.
For you will spread out to the right and to the left;
    your descendants will dispossess nations
    and settle in their desolate cities."

ISAIAH 54:1–3, NIV

First comes increasing pressure and a growing awareness that something must change. Then comes outright desperation, followed often by an encounter with the transforming power of God. After another waiting period (when people try to take things into their own hands) and a time of travail (when patience wears thin) comes the new birth. Subsequent to the new birth, growth and expansion can explode.

Because God is preparing to do a new thing in the earth, He is stirring up a vast chorus of cries. Although He needs to destroy old structures in order to build new ones, He is not looking for people to join Him as demolition warriors as much as He is looking for vessels for His new wine. God is provoking movement and flow; He is assembling a presence-driven people whose collective authority and forward movement will rewrite history. He is looking for a people who will not only drink the wine of His Spirit, but who will buy up the wine store, so to speak, so that they can pour out His wine to the world. On their own, they will need to abandon their reliance on the old structures, but the Kingdom flow will take care of washing those away.

God always sends out the prophetic voices first. John the Baptist preceded Jesus. Prophetic voices announce, prepare, set up and sensitize people to what God is getting ready to do. As the Word of the Lord flows, some get offended with the flow and want it to stop. But it will only increase in intensity until the prophesied new thing breaks out at last.

Free to Flow

Moses cried out, saying that unless God's presence went with His people, they would not go up (see Exodus 33:15). At that point, he was not worried about the Egyptian government or the institution of slavery that kept his people in bondage. He knew that God's presence would effect all necessary changes, regardless of how impossible they seemed. He knew he needed the presence of God, which would make a way.

God's all-powerful presence comes to reside in places where

intense, insatiable hunger and thirst have caused people to seek Him. Jeremiah wrote:

> You will seek Me and find Me, when you search for Me with all your heart. I will be found by you, says the LORD, and I will bring you back from your captivity; I will gather you from all the nations and from all the places where I have driven you, says the LORD, and I will bring you to the place from which I cause you to be carried away captive.
>
> *JEREMIAH 29:13–14*

Wherever God comes, freedom breaks out. "Now the Lord is the Spirit; and where the Spirit of the Lord is, there is liberty" (2 Corinthians 3:17). Rigid rules get set aside. Joyful flexibility holds sway.

Sometimes I wonder if Pentecost could have happened in some of our rule-bound churches today. Why do we teach people to hear God's voice and then restrict them from sharing what He has said unless they are inside the church building with an elder listening? When those 120 believers ran out of that Upper Room, there is no telling what they might have said to people. God's power is big enough to allow for exceptional flexibility.

When God moves in a new outpouring, He moves both downward vertically and outward horizontally. Those spontaneous Pentecost sermons reached the whole world eventually. God's new strategy depended on only one thing—the ever-flowing river of His Spirit. Like any river, it shifted and turned, picked things up and then dropped them, ebbed and flowed fast and slow as it affected generations of people.

This may seem extreme to some, but miraculous and unusual occurrences will happen all along the way in a new time. People will get healed. They might go into trances. They might shake and quake as old structures break off. They will get reconstituted and infused with new capabilities. Anything can happen. Once when a friend of mine was visiting a church, God's presence came and it began to rain inside the building. It really happened, but you had to witness it to believe it. It created an amazing, awe-filled shout to the King of all kings.

What Is Your Place?

Each of us is free to decide how much to participate in the move of God. In other words, you can open to the first page of your new book in this new era and write "N/A"—for "Not Applicable," "Not Available" or maybe "No Answer." If you are so inclined, you can leave your new book completely blank.

But I am assuming you do not want to do that. I am assuming you want to align yourself with God's activity and ally yourself with His Spirit in one or more of His many moves. Who and what you line yourself up with will affect the anointing that falls on you. Ruth aligned herself with Naomi in the midst of her mourning. From that alignment came Ruth's future, her inheritance, her resources and her connections for posterity. She followed Naomi to Bethlehem, which became their place of visitation from God. Your alignments should lead you to fresh God-encounters, too.

As you change from a Church paradigm to a Kingdom paradigm, listen to Jesus. Jesus told His disciples to go about teaching and preaching the Gospel of the Kingdom and doing the works of the Kingdom. The works of the Kingdom will be a little different for each of us. You must find your element and flow in it. What are you good at? What do you love to do? How is God heightening your sense of calling? You may not hear literal words that define your assignment, but as you "go with the flow" of the Spirit in your life, you will find out more about how you fit into the big picture of the Kingdom.

If you are about to shift into a new gear, you do not want to make the same mistakes you may have made in the past. Evaluate yourself.

143

What needs to change on the inside so that you will not repeat the same "people mistakes" such as taking up offenses, compromising in sinful relationships, lacking personal awareness or displaying character weaknesses? Determine whether or not you have repented for missing the mark in the past. Figure out what you need to fix or make right yourself and what you must depend on God to do.

Remember that God Himself is the source of your strength. Savor your God-encounters and do whatever you can to get closer to Him. Remember that "those who wait on the LORD shall renew their strength" (Isaiah 40:31). In your Kingdom adventures to come, even the hidden exploits you do will require supernatural strength.

Time for the New Book

We have entered a time of increasing uncertainty, a time where danger, fears and anxiety increase. Yet for us as believers, it is a time when heaven is closer to us than ever before. The closer we get to the end, the greater will be the outpouring of the Holy Spirit.

As you enter this new season with a new book in your hands, you will write your story with your life (and sometimes with words) about your exploits, as well as about your thoughts, longings, observations, experiences, failures and successes. With the steps you take each day, you will record everything that is about to unfold. The text of your book will form out of the vision or assignment that God gives you. It will be influenced by your ministry skills and your gifts, what you witness, the testimonies that unfold around you and the evidences of God's heart of compassion as He salvages a dying world and makes it fit for the Kingdom.

Whether you are writing this new book with your life, with your pen or with both, at least four main themes will guide you: (1) the experience of your freedom to *be* the Bride, (2) the resulting new empowerment and release to do the works of Jesus, (3) the end-time revival and awakening, and (4) the wonders of the all-conquering Kingdom of God.

Childlikeness will mark every page you live out as you write with a sense of pure wonderment, joyful adventure, loving abandon, trust and simple faith. With the turning of each page, Kingdom advances will emerge. Your book will record what caused you to seek first the Kingdom of God, when and how that happened and where that search carried you. Between the lines, you will see how the Kingdom works, how it brings with it an ongoing experience of righteousness, peace and joy in the Holy Spirit (see Romans 14:17).

Unlike most people around you, you will not view trouble, persecution or tribulation as problems. In fact, you will consider them transformational because they are your ticket to the Kingdom. As Acts 14:22 says, "We must through many tribulations enter the kingdom of God." You will be prepared for revival on a large scale when it comes, because you will have become accustomed to persevering prayer, which is required beforehand to release the revival and afterward to propel it forward with intensity. You will be used as an instrument of salvation and harvest. You will attain the physical, emotional and spiritual strength required, because God's Spirit will supply all that you need. You will be prepared to intervene in difficult situations with new and unusual strategies. You will be flexible. Your earnest attentiveness to God's direction will make it possible for Him to infiltrate pockets of darkness that have never before seen His light.

When read alongside the pages of others' books, the pages of your life will show that you were part of the Church, the Bride. You were called out of the culture, ethnicity, gender and nationality into which you were born to be part of the people of God's Kingdom. Your book will show that your identity and worldview were formed by heaven and not by earth, by God and not by the god of this world.

You will see along the way that you are becoming a person who possesses a sure faith in the midst of uncertainty, holding up faith, hope and charity in the midst of fear and betrayal. As the chapters of your book add up, you will be able to trace the advance of the Kingdom. Little by little, the kingdoms of this world will be conquered as you combine your efforts with the efforts of others, moving from multiplying and bearing fruit to subduing and taking dominion.

You will become confident in your identity as part of the Bride, marked by beauty and purity, betrothed to the Bridegroom and destined for the Garden, designed to rule and reign with Christ, even in this life. You will experience the wrath of the one who stands against the Bride, the Harlot whose husband is the devil, but you will be confident that their contentions will not prove successful.

Your book will end well because the Kingdom endures and overcomes. You are now writing part of a bigger story, and your participation in the story will be your greatest achievement. Out of your desperate cries to heaven, each a cry that God hears, will have come the help that you needed. As you graduate, you will throw your book up toward heaven with the victory cry. In the end, your cry will echo Christ's own: "It is finished!"

NOTES

CHAPTER ONE: THE DILEMMA

1. See Joshua Cooper Ramo, *The Age of the Unthinkable: Why the New World Disorder Constantly Surprises Us and What We Can Do about It* (New York: Little, Brown and Co., 2009), 10.
2. Ibid., 9.

CHAPTER TWO: THE NEW BOOK

1. *Nelson's New Illustrated Bible Dictionary* (Nashville: Thomas Nelson Publishers, 1995, 1986), s.v. "Jasher, Book of," as found at http://www.ebible.com/dict/NNIBD/nnibd-03324.

CHAPTER FOUR: CHANGE, WHETHER YOU LIKE IT OR NOT

1. Pesi Fonua (AP), "Pacific Quake Could Mean More Eruptions," *AOL News,* March 20, 2009, http://www.aolnews.com/.
2. Brown, Driver, Briggs, and Gesenius, *The Old Testament Hebrew Lexicon,* s.v. "chadash" (Strong's #2319), http://www.searchgodsword.org/lex/heb/view.cgi?number=02319.
3. Frank Viola, "What's Wrong with Our Gospel?", *Emergent Village Weblog,* March 16, 2009, http://www.emergentvillage.com/weblog/whats-wrong-with-our-gospel.

CHAPTER SIX: DESPERATELY UNCERTAIN

1. "Emotional and Psychological Trauma: Causes and Effects, Symptoms and Treatment," *HealingResources.info* (sponsored by the Santa Barbara

Graduate Institute Center for Clinical Studies and Research and L.A. County Early Identification and Intervention Group), http://www .healingresources.info/emotional_trauma_overview.htm#3.

2. Ibid.

3. Ibid.

CHAPTER SEVEN: FIND YOUR DOOR

1. *Biblesoft's New Exhaustive Strong's Numbers and Concordance with Expanded Greek-Hebrew Dictionary* (Biblesoft and International Bible Translators, Inc., 1994, 2003, 2006), s.v.v. "caph" (*Strong's* #5592), "caphaph" (*Strong's* #5605).

2. Brown, Driver, Briggs, and Gesenius, *The Old Testament Hebrew Lexicon*, s.v.v. "miphtan" (*Strong's* #4670), http://www.searchgodsword.org/ lex/heb/view.cgi?number=04670, "pethen" (*Strong's* #6620), http:// www.searchgodsword.org/lex/heb/view.cgi?number=06620.

3. Barbara J. Yoder, *The Breaker Anointing* (Colorado Springs: Wagner Publications, 2001), 51.

4. Brown, Driver, Briggs, and Gesenius, *Old Testament Hebrew Lexicon*, s.v.v. "pethach" (*Strong's* #6607), http://www.searchgodsword.org/lex/ heb/view.cgi?number=06607, "pathach" (*Strong's* #6605), http://www .searchgodsword.org/lex/heb/view.cgi?number=06605.

CHAPTER EIGHT: THE CRY

1. This account has been verified by my friend Patricia Beall Gruits, now in her eighties, daughter of Myrtle Beall, and by the "History" section of the website of Bethesda Christian Church (formerly Bethesda Missionary Temple) in Sterling Heights, Michigan, http://www .bethesdachristian.org/362002.ihtml.

2. J. Edwin Orr, an Oxford-educated church historian, gave a talk in 1976 at the national Prayer Congress in Dallas. It was entitled "The Role of Prayer in Spiritual Awakening." An excerpt from a transcript of the talk describes the revival that followed the Fulton Street prayer meetings:

> In February and March of 1858, every church and public hall in downtown New York was filled. Horace Greeley, the famous editor, sent a reporter with horse and buggy racing around the prayer meetings to see how many men were praying: in one hour, he could get to only twelve meetings, but

he counted 6100 men attending. Then a landslide of prayer began, which overflowed to the churches in the evenings. People began to be converted, ten thousand a week in New York City alone. The movement spread throughout New England, the church bells bringing people to prayer at eight in the morning, twelve noon, six in the evening.

SCRIPTURE INDEX

153

ABOUT THE AUTHOR

BARBARA J. YODER is the apostolic leader of Shekinah in Ann Arbor, Michigan. Shekinah is an apostolic and prophetic church with a multiracial, multicultural constituency. Barbara believes the Church must engage God's presence to see the release of God's breakthrough power, which affects and ultimately transforms both people and territories locally, regionally and internationally. She puts a strong value on the centrality of the presence of God, the Word, prayer and worship in the life of the Church. She believes the Church is not a building but a people, called to move out of the four walls and into the marketplace (government, business, education), with a passion to transform the world, one person at a time. And she never forgets that Jesus loved people and was called a friend of sinners. (Visit www.shekinahchurch.org for more information.)

Besides serving as the apostolic leader of Shekinah, Barbara has mobilized a network of leaders called Breakthrough Apostolic Ministries Network (BAM). BAM has four divisions that equip, train and support leaders of churches, businesses and government, intercessory and ministry leaders. She has a call to business and government leaders for the purpose of transformation—supporting them in releasing the Kingdom of God in the marketplace, as well as developing new paradigms and nurturing an innovative atmosphere that enables them to change with the times and seasons.

A third endeavor of Barbara's is Breakthrough Leadership Institute, a regional equipping and training program to assist individuals to fulfill their call not only in the church but also the marketplace. Barbara believes that the core anointing of an apostolic people is breakthrough, enabling them to overcome every hindrance and obstacle, thereby ushering in God's transforming power. Further, the strategic release of breakthrough knowledge, power and wisdom must arise out of a prophetic heart and spirit.

Barbara has an abiding passion to connect with like-minded leaders in the church, business, government and education across regions, states and nations. Above all, Barbara has a passion for God, for people and for life, which has been forged out of years of experience with both the triumphs and challenges of real life. In addition to *The Cry God Hears*, Barbara has authored other books to help people grow into the fullness of who they are in Christ. These include *The Overcomer's Anointing* (Chosen, 2009), *Taking on Goliath* (Charisma House, 2009), *God's Bold Call to Women* (Regal Books, 2005) and *The Breaker Anointing* (Regal Books, 2004).

Barbara values authenticity, combined with a down-to-earth and practical approach to life and ministry. Her own life experiences include teaching in several universities, building a church from the ground up, interacting with many churches, leaders and ministries across the world, and being married, as well as facing the death of her husband. Through it all, she has learned to value realness. Barbara believes that an untested Christian life that has not come through difficulties victoriously lacks genuineness.

For more information about Shekinah Christian Church, Breakthrough Apostolic Ministries Network (BAM) and Breakthrough

Leadership Institute, as well as other resources available from Barbara J. Yoder, visit www.shekinahchurch.org. To contact Barbara, write or call:

Shekinah
4600 Scio Church Road
Ann Arbor, Michigan 48103
Telephone: (734) 662-6040
Fax: (734) 662-5470
Email: pastorbarbara@shekinahchurch.org
Subcribe to her blog at www.barbarayoderblog.com.